# Cambridge Elements ≡

**Elements in Forensic Linguistics**
edited by
Tim Grant
*Aston University*
Tammy Gales
*Hofstra University*

# SPOKEN THREATS FROM PRODUCTION TO PERCEPTION

James Tompkinson
*University of York*

**CAMBRIDGE**
UNIVERSITY PRESS

## CAMBRIDGE
### UNIVERSITY PRESS

Shaftesbury Road, Cambridge CB2 8EA, United Kingdom

One Liberty Plaza, 20th Floor, New York, NY 10006, USA

477 Williamstown Road, Port Melbourne, VIC 3207, Australia

314–321, 3rd Floor, Plot 3, Splendor Forum, Jasola District Centre,
New Delhi – 110025, India

103 Penang Road, #05–06/07, Visioncrest Commercial, Singapore 238467

Cambridge University Press is part of Cambridge University Press & Assessment,
a department of the University of Cambridge.

We share the University's mission to contribute to society through the pursuit of
education, learning and research at the highest international levels of excellence.

www.cambridge.org
Information on this title: www.cambridge.org/9781009494496

DOI: 10.1017/9781009292986

First published 2023

*A catalogue record for this publication is available from the British Library*

ISBN 978-1-009-49449-6 Hardback
ISBN 978-1-009-29301-3 Paperback
ISSN 2634-7334 (online)
ISSN 2634-7326 (print)

# Spoken Threats from Production to Perception

Elements in Forensic Linguistics

DOI: 10.1017/9781009292986
First published online: December 2023

James Tompkinson
*University of York*

**Author for correspondence:** James Tompkinson, james.tompkinson@york.ac.uk

**Abstract**: Spoken threats are a common but linguistically complex language crime. Although threatening language has been examined from different linguistic perspectives, there is limited research which critically addresses how people perceive spoken threats and infer traits such as threat and intent from speakers' voices. There is also minimal linguistic research addressing differences between written and spoken threats. By specifically analysing threats delivered in both written and spoken modalities, as well as integrating perceptual phonetic analysis into discussions on spoken threats, this Element offers perspectives on these two under-researched areas. It highlights the dangers of assuming that the way in which someone sounds correlates with, for example, their intention to commit harm, and explores potential problems in assuming that written and spoken threats are equivalent to one another. The goal of the Element is to advance linguistic knowledge and understanding around spoken threats, as well as promote further research in the area.

**Keywords:** forensic linguistics, speech perception, language crimes, threats, language and law

ISBNs: 9781009494496 (HB), 9781009293013 (PB), 9781009292986 (OC)
ISSNs: 2634-7334 (online), 2634-7326 (print)

# Contents

## Series Preface

The Elements in Forensic Linguistics series from Cambridge University Press publishes across four main topic areas (1) investigative and forensic text analysis; (2) the study of spoken linguistic practices in legal contexts; (3) the linguistic analysis of written legal texts; (4) explorations of the origins, development, and scope of the field in various countries and regions. *Spoken Threats from Production to Perception* by James Tompkinson is situated in the second of these categories and presents results from a series of corpus-based and experimental studies that investigate how verbal threats and 'a threatening tone of voice' are both produced and perceived in a variety of contexts.

As an academic working in the field of forensic phonetics, James Tompkinson brings a balanced perspective to the analysis of spoken threats. Drawing on categories proposed by French and Watt (2018), Tompkinson explains that previous work on spoken threats has largely been *responsive* in nature. That is, it has occurred in response to a research question posed to address a particular forensic case. In this Element, Tompkinson provides much-needed research from an *anticipatory* perspective. That is, research that investigates questions with potential for real-world applications in a wide variety of contexts, including forensic cases.

Thus, the contents of this Element provide several important contributions to the study of threatening communications. First, Tompkinson introduces us to a new Corpus of Spoken Threats (CoST), which is now available for further research purposes upon request to the author; second, he provides a comparison of the linguistic features produced in written vs spoken threats using existing literature on written threats and findings from the new CoST corpus; and third, he offers a synthesis of recent experimental work on the perception of spoken threats, furthering our understanding of what a threat actually is and how they are perceived. We hope this innovative work will encourage additional research on this context-based language crime.

Tammy Gales
Series Editor

## Prologue

In the time, I have spent conducting academic research, I have often found that some of the most interesting projects begin almost by accident. One example of this is how the research on which this contribution to the Elements in Forensic Linguistics Series is based came to exist. In the autumn of 2013, I had just finished my undergraduate degree in English Language and Linguistics at the University of York. Around this time, I met with Dominic Watt in the back bar of the York

Brewery pub to discuss postgraduate study options. Dom happened to mention a criminal case that he was aware of, where the use of a so-termed 'threatening tone of voice' was a factor in a custody officer perceiving a spoken utterance from a detainee as a reiteration of a threat to kill. At first mention, this seemed unproblematic to me; a threat delivered in a threatening tone of voice. So what? But it quickly became apparent that Dom and I could not begin to distil what a 'threatening tone of voice' would be in terms of definable features of speech. As our discussion progressed, we questioned whether it was even possible to define what a 'threatening tone of voice' was, despite its existence in common parlance, or how spoken threats might differ from threats delivered in written form. In fact, our only source of agreement was that this topic required further research, and that it would take a team of researchers with equal interest in both forensic linguistics and forensic phonetics to undertake the task. Over the coming years, Dom would supervise both me and Sarah Kelly as we pursued MSc and PhD research into the language of spoken threats and tried to set about addressing some of the questions we had about this common type of language crime. The aim of this Element is to provide some of the answers to those questions we first posed nearly 10 years ago.

## 1 Introduction

In 2015, the UK Parliamentary Office of Science and Technology produced a report entitled 'Forensic Language Analysis' (Bunn and Foxen, 2015). This report was designed to provide an introductory and accessible review of research conducted in the academic fields of forensic linguistics and forensic speech science, aimed at a non-specialist audience. The authors of the report provide a review of different topics including authorship analysis, speaker comparison and transcription. They also highlight the scepticism and concerns that forensic phoneticians have raised over claims that the voice can be used as a tool for procedures such as deception detection. However, the most interesting part of the report for readers of this Element was the observation of a disjointed relationship between non-linguists (in this case jurors) and linguistic experts. The authors state that 'jurors expect certain procedures to be possible which experts assert are not, such as personality analysis, determining truth and falsity, and assessing threat in speech intonation (although this is a research interest)' (Bunn and Foxen, 2015: 3).

Bunn and Foxen's (2015) report highlights that non-linguists believe that it is possible for linguistic experts to do things that they cannot in relation to certain aspects of language analysis, including in the analysis of spoken threats. Indeed, a question I am frequently asked when I tell non-linguists that I work in forensic speech science is 'does that mean you can tell if someone is lying from their voice?'. If I am ever asked to explain my work on spoken threats, non-linguists will often ask 'so does that mean you can tell the police when a threat is serious based on the way that someone speaks?'. The idea that experts could be asked to make such important, categorical decisions based on voice and speech patterns alone is, of course, unrealistic. However, the expectation from non-linguists that these kinds of decisions can be made by language experts (not helped by fictional TV programmes which show 'experts' making *exactly* these kinds of decisions), is highly problematic because it creates a disparity between non-linguistic expectations and linguistic reality.

Having considered this key misconception about the work of the forensic linguist in relation to spoken threats, it is equally important to examine what forensic linguists *can* offer to the study of threatening language. To do this, we must first consider where the study of threats falls within the overall field of forensic linguistics. In their textbook 'An Introduction to Forensic Linguistics: Language in Evidence', Coulthard, Johnson and Wright (2017) break the field down into two broad categories. The first of these is 'The Language of the Legal Process', which covers areas such as the language of the law, courtrooms and police interviews. The second, 'Language as Evidence', focusses on areas such as authorship attribution, forensic phonetics, plagiarism detection, and expert witness evidence. This split is similar to both Larner's (2015) and Nini's (2019) discussions of 'descriptive' and 'investigative' forensic linguistics. Generally speaking, a distinction can be drawn between work which describes linguistic phenomena which have forensic relevance, and work which provides evidential linguistic analysis to assist criminal or civil trials.

Coulthard, Johnson and Wright (2017) provide one of the most comprehensive overviews of forensic linguistics as an academic discipline, and yet it is not automatically clear where the analysis of threats should be placed within the two broad areas of forensic linguistics that they propose. This is arguably because the linguistic analysis of threatening language transcends the boundary between these research areas, depending on the particular question being asked. Perhaps a more useful categorisation for research on spoken threats is the split between 'anticipatory' and 'responsive' research, as discussed by French and Watt (2018) in relation to research impact. French and Watt (2018: 153) categorise anticipatory research as research that has potential for real-world applications but doesn't respond directly to a specific case or an urgent, immediate need for data. Contrastingly, responsive research does the opposite and aims to answer a specific question about a specific case through linguistic research or analysis. Relating this to the study of threatening language, general research on threats as a type of language crime would be largely *anticipatory*, whereas attempting to use linguistic research to help answer (or provide legitimate reasons not to answer) questions such as 'is this particular utterance a threat?' would be *responsive*. However, in order to answer a specific question about a particular threatening utterance, it is essential to understand how threats work at a more general level. In other words, we need anticipatory research to be able to respond appropriately to specific questions about threatening language.

I first encountered this issue in 2016, when I was asked to write an article for *The Conversation* about spoken threats. The request for this article came following news that a series of hoax bomb threats had been made to schools across the United Kingdom.[1] Rather than comment on the specifics of this case in a completely responsive way, I opted to discuss why, following research which showed that there are no consistent phonetic cues to deception (see, e.g., Kirchhübel, 2013), attempting to identify whether a threat was a hoax or not based on a speaker's voice was unrealistic. I also discussed some research which highlighted why threat perception based on a speaker's voice can be linked to unhelpful linguistic stereotypes. My concluding words in that article were as follows:

> *Just because a listener may be inclined to think a speaker sounds more threatening based on different aspects of their voice, there is no basis to say this makes a speaker any more likely to commit any action they threaten. And the less we rely on stereotyped impressions of speech in potentially high-stakes situations, the better.* (Tompkinson, 2016)

The work in this Element has been designed to offer more research to help expand on the kinds of issues I first discussed in the above article. The work presented here should, according to French and Watt's (2018) definitions, be classed as anticipatory rather than responsive research. The work in this Element does not respond to a specific problem or case, but instead presents more general analyses to help illuminate areas of interest and contribute to knowledge about threatening language. Of course, my contribution here is far from the first in this area. Linguistic research on threatening language stretches back several decades and offers many complimentary and contrasting perspectives. This existing body of research is discussed and evaluated in Section 2, but there are two specific aspects which I argue are under-researched and where this Element provides a more specific contribution.

The first of these under-researched areas concerns the treatment of spoken and written threats. The balance of research on threatening language is much more heavily weighted towards the written modality. There are also some studies which, while offering useful perspectives on the topic, do not

---

[1] https://theconversation.com/bomb-scares-can-you-judge-a-threat-from-the-voice-on-the-phone-60073

separate spoken threats from written ones. This area is identified by Gales (2021) as an area which requires further research, and Section 3 of this Element addresses this directly. I firstly present an analysis of key linguistic features within a newly created spoken threat corpus followed by a comparative analysis with previous research on written threats. The work in Section 3 begins to bridge the gap between linguistic research on threats delivered in the two modalities, while also contributing to our understanding of the similarities and differences between spoken and written threats in a way which has not yet been done.

The second under-researched area that this Element addresses is whether the way in which a spoken threat is uttered can affect perceptions of the speaker. In Section 4, I describe a programme of experimental research which was conducted to critically examine how both speech and speaker factors can contribute to someone being perceived as sounding threatening. This ties into the notion of a 'threatening tone of voice' and whether there is a linguistic or phonetic basis for such a label. I also highlight both the strengths and weaknesses of experimental research which examines perceptions of spoken threats, as well as the dangers of directly applying experimental results to specific legally relevant situations.

The overall aim of this contribution to the Elements in Forensic Linguistics series is to advance knowledge and promote further debate over the central question of what we can, and perhaps more importantly what we cannot, say about threatening language.

## 2 Threatening Language: A Research Review

### 2.1 Defining Threats

Threats form a substantial part of our everyday language use. There are many possible reasons why a speaker may threaten someone, and we all make threats from time-to-time to achieve a specific course of action. In most cases, these kinds of everyday threats do not express any criminal intent and are not illegal. Consider a mother who threatens her child that their favourite toy will be taken away unless the child puts their shoes on and leaves the house quickly. Although this interaction is not illegal, a clear threat is made by the mother towards her child in the guise of 'if you don't do the thing I want you to do [put shoes on and leave the house] then something bad will happen [a toy will be taken away]'. Another example of an authentic but non-illegal threat, discussed by Solan and Tiersma (2015: 223), is of a boss threatening an employee that they will be fired if they do something wrong at work. The use of threats in everyday language brings together the notions of actions and consequences, binding language use to a person's ability to ensure that unfavourable things can happen if certain conditions are not met. Storey (1995: 74) goes as far as to say that threats are simply 'a way of life', with Milburn and Watman (1981: 2) commenting that they provide speakers with a way of exerting personal and social control in unpredictable situations or environments.

However, when threats become illegal, they can serve as both standalone crimes and form part of other serious crimes such as robbery and extortion (Yamanaka, 1995: 38). Solan and Tiersma (2015: 224) state that threats are often used to accomplish serious crimes, with Greenawalt (1989: 92) also explaining that criminal acts frequently involve threats which aim to get an innocent victim to commit to an unfavourable course of action. Threats can also be illegal if they are directed towards certain people, such as the President of the United States (Danet et al., 1980) or members of the United Kingdom's royal family (Solan and Tiersma, 2015: 233). The dual nature of threats as standalone crimes and as an integral part of other crimes is captured by the definition of 'threat' provided by the Oxford Dictionary of Law (Law and Martin, 2009), which states that a threat is 'the expression of an intention to harm someone with the object of forcing them to do something' and that threats are 'an ingredient of many crimes'. The Oxford Dictionary of Law provides a more detailed definition for 'threatening behaviour', which is listed as the use of 'threatening, abusive or insulting words or behaviour' towards another person (Law and Martin, 2009). The statement and expression of intention in a threat is sufficient to uphold its status as a threat, even if the speaker has no actual intention to carry out the threatened action. One example of this is the case of Seif Eldin Mustafa, who hijacked EgyptAir flight MS181 in March 2016 and threatened to blow up the aircraft using a belt containing explosives (BBC News, 2016). It was subsequently revealed that the belt contained no explosives and therefore Mustafa could never have intended to blow up the aircraft, but the threat was considered real by security staff and those on board the plane and was therefore valid.

Despite such definitions, Gales (2016: 3) has previously warned that there is a lack of understanding about what threatening language 'actually is', and of the potential dangers when those tasked with assessing linguistic aspects of threats rely on personal or stereotypical assumptions rather than evidence-based approaches. This potential problem is further compounded when the modality of a threat is spoken rather than written. Spoken threats provide an additional problem in that unless a recording of a threatening utterance exists, they are momentary and are therefore more heavily reliant on listeners' perceptions of the speaker's intentions. There is also something of a shortage of research examining how spoken threats are perceived by listeners (Watt, Kelly and

Llamas, 2013), although some steps have been taken in more recent years to address this (e.g., Kelly, 2018; Tompkinson, 2018; Tompkinson et al., 2023).

There are several cases which highlight the need for further research into listener evaluations of spoken threats. One such example is documented in Watt, Kelly and Llamas (2013) and comes from a 2012 crown court trial where the defendant was accused of reiterating a previously unrecorded threat to kill by uttering the words '*I will do summat* [a northern English dialect term for 'something'] *about it when I get out and it won't be with guns or anything like that*'. This utterance was produced following a situation where the defendant had been held in a police cell and was remonstrating to a custody officer that he wanted to be released. This custody officer was the hearer of the alleged reiteration of the previous unrecorded threat to kill.

This case provides one example of what Gales (2010) terms an indirect threat, where a threat is judged to have been uttered, yet the wording of the utterance does not explicitly signal intent-to-harm on the part of the speaker. Indirect threats do not overtly make clear that a threat is being made, and could, on wording alone, be classified as other types of speech acts including warnings, insults, complaints or promises. In the example above, the vague nature of the phrase '*I will do summat about it*' meant that listener interpretation was required to determine what that 'something' was, and by extension whether the speaker had criminal intentions or not. The interpretation that '*I will do summat about it when I get out and it won't be with guns or anything like that*' constituted a serious threat would require listener inference of the speaker's intentions. The speaker's words in this case, if taken in their most literal interpretation, specifically ruled out the use of guns or similar weapons, and yet the utterance was still interpreted as a reiteration of a serious death threat. Watt, Kelly and Llamas (2013) also point out that during the subsequent trial, the custody officer's testimony identified that the defendant's behaviour, the surrounding context and the fact that he used an aggressive tone of voice, served as evidence which supported the interpretation of the utterance in question as a serious threat.

Another example where perceptions of a speaker's voice had a role a trial involving spoken threats is taken from the Danish Supreme Court (case number U.2016.1939 H – TfK2016.491H)[2]. In this case, a man was accused of threatening to cut a fellow employee's throat. As part of the defence, the accused threatener stated that because he had a low-pitched voice, he was often perceived as sounding angry. The translated and original text from the court report is produced below:

[2] I am grateful to Professor Tanya Karoli Christensen for alerting me to this case, and for providing the relevant background information and translations.

**English**

*The defendant is very careful with how he phrases things since he is some-times misunderstood and perceived as angry because he has a very deep voice. He never raises his voice since nothing good comes from it anyway. He can, however, be somewhat direct in his demeanour.*

**Danish**

*Tiltalte passer meget på, hvordan han formulerer sig, idet han sommertider bliver misforstået og opfattet som sur fordi han har en meget dyb stemme. Han hæver aldrig stemmen, da man sjældent får noget ud af det alligevel. Han kan dog somme tider godt være lidt kontant i sin fremtræden.*

Here, the defendant's perception of his own voice was offered as a mitigating circumstance in court. Furthermore, throughout the case, the defendant was described by the hearer of the threat as sounding both angry and frustrated. Ultimately in this case, the defendant was found guilty and sentenced to a fine and 30 days imprisonment. But this example does highlight the complexity of using aspects of voice as evidence in criminal trials involving spoken threats.

## 2.2 Types of Threats

Shuy (1993) classifies a threat as a type of language crime. There are two broad types of verbal threats: direct and indirect (Gales, 2010). A direct threat overtly states that something unfavourable will happen and potentially also include information about the time, place and people that will be involved in the threatened action. By contrast, indirect threats are more problematic because they involve the speaker communicating more information than is contained in the words alone (Searle, 1979: 30). The potential for misinterpretation or misunderstanding is heightened when indirect threats are made, owing to a lack of expressed clarity on the part of the speaker.

Consider, for example, an utterance such as '*I know where you live*'. Based on wording alone, there is no expression of intention to perform an unfavourable act. However, as Watt, Kelly and Llamas (2013) discuss, the utterance could plausibly be interpreted as a threat given the right context and conditions. Sentences of every type of syntactic form can count as indirect threats (Fraser, 1998: 169), and these are often masked as other type of speech acts including questions ('*Are you sure you want to do that?*'), promises ('*I promise you'll get what's coming to you*'), and warnings ('*I'm warning you, I'll never forget this*').

It is also possible for utterances like those detailed above to have multiple interpretations. Take an utterance like '*Are you sure you want to do that?*'. If interpreted literally, this would be a question which would evoke a yes/no response from the hearer. However, it could equally be used to warn if the goal is not to question the hearer but rather to get them to reflect on whether to do something potentially unfavourable. It could also be used as a threat if the unfavourable action was to be performed by the speaker to the hearer's detriment. With these kinds of utterances, the interpretation is left for the hearer to infer. Additionally, Searle (1979: 7) points out that speakers very rarely threaten by stating 'I threaten X', where 'threaten' is used performatively. This contrasts with warnings and promises, where it is perfectly plausible to declare 'I warn/ promise X'.

However, despite the categorisation of threats as either direct or indirect, there is a great deal of fluidity both within and between the two categories. Consider, for example, the two hypothetical examples of potential threat utterances, below.

> *I'm warning you about a bomb at York Station. It will go off this afternoon.*
> *I know where you live.*

Both utterances can be classified as indirect threats. The first could be classified as an indirect threat owing to the possible interpretations as either a warning or a threat, depending on the speaker's intention. Gales (2017, personal communication) classifies this type of utterance as a direct performative warning, but an indirect threat. If the utterance is interpreted literally, then it is a direct and clear warning owing to the use of 'warn' as a performative verb, whereas the threat interpretation requires listener inference as to the speaker's intentions. The speaker could simply argue that they are providing a warning which was helpful to the hearer, rather than threatening something unfavourable. However, given the severity of the action mentioned (a bomb exploding) and the mention of a clear time and a place, this utterance is more direct than 'I know where you live'. An utterance such as 'I know where you live' clearly requires a greater level of listener inference to arrive at a threat interpretation. The labelling of a threat as either direct or indirect can be seen as a method of to provide a base level of classification, with more nuanced and fluid classifications present within these overarching categories.

One such sub-category within the umbrella classifications of 'direct' and 'indirect' is the conditional threat. Both direct and indirect threats can be worded conditionally, and these types of threats are created through the incorporation of a conditionality clause into the wording (Gales, 2010: 9). Linguistically, this conditionality can be expressed in various ways but commonly takes a form such as 'if you don't do X, then I will do Y' (Milburn and Watman, 1981: 11), 'do X and we won't do Y' or 'do X or I'll do Y'.

The use of conditionality within the wording of threats relates to the relative position and control of both speakers and hearers. When there is no conditionality clause in the wording of a threat, the speaker presents information and the listener has no control over the outcome. The speaker therefore remains in the position of power over the threatened action throughout. A hypothetical example of this would be an utterance such as '*I'm going to kill you*', where if the speaker has the intention to commit the threatened action, there is nothing in the wording of the utterance that gives any control to the recipient. Contrast this utterance with a conditional version of the same direct threat – '*If you don't pay me the money I'm owed, I'm going to kill you*'- and the message in the utterance becomes somewhat ambiguous. The conditionality suggests that the purpose of the utterance is to get the hearer to pay the owed money to the speaker. However, as Gales (2010: 11) correctly points out, just because a speaker factors a condition into the design of their threat, there is no obligation on the speaker's part to adhere to the stated condition. This is because the speaker remains in a position of power over the hearer throughout. However, for a conditional threat to be successfully communicated, the target of the threat must believe that either the stated unfavourable action will not take place if they agree to the condition, or that the chances of avoiding the unfavourable action will be increased as a result of compliance with the condition. Taking the example provided above, this would mean that the addressee believes that if they pay the money, then the speaker is less likely to, or will not, commit the act of killing. The key factor for conditional threats is, therefore, whether the addressee believes they have control over the outcome, rather than whether they actually have any control or not.

## 2.3 The Roles of Speakers and Hearers in Threat Communication

In their review of a series of cases involving threats made towards the President of the United States, Danet, Hoffman and Kermish (1980) show that the majority of judgements rested on the so-called 'reasonable person' test. This is that if a reasonable person would interpret an utterance as a threat, then a threat has been made. However, the 'reasonable person' notion is rejected by Gingiss (1986) on the grounds that it does not attempt to define a threat, nor does it highlight the grounds upon which a so-called 'reasonable person' would interpret an utterance as being threatening. Furthermore, it is legitimate to question what a 'reasonable person' is, and what criteria would qualify someone as being 'reasonable' in the context of threat perception. Gingiss (1986: 153) argues that the assumption that both a speaker and a hearer will 'know a threat when they hear one' is insufficient for courtroom purposes, despite its status as 'the majority view'. These issues are particularly problematic with respect to indirect threats, which require a greater amount of interpretation on the part of the hearer than is required for direct threats. This is specifically addressed by Gingiss (1986: 155), who argues that 'the problem of indirect threats is one that the courts must deal with'.

In an attempt to better define indirect threats, Gingiss (1986) applies Labov and Fanshel's (1977) framework for the classification of indirect requests to Fraser's (1975) framework for threat classification. The resulting conditions for defining indirect threats are:

> *If A makes an assertion to be about:*
>
> a. *the existential status of an action p*
> b. *the time, T, of a future action p*
> c. *other preconditions for a valid threat as given in the rule of threats (see Fraser, 1975)*
>
> *and all other preconditions are in effect, then A is heard as making a valid threat.* (Gingiss, 1986)

Gingiss (1986: 156) argues that a framework such as this allows for utterances like 'this gun is loaded' to be classified as a threat, given that the utterance indirectly asserts the speaker's ability to shoot the gun. However, such a statement could be interpreted differently depending on the shared under-standing between speaker and hearer over the meaning of the utterance and the situation in which it was uttered. In a critique of Gingiss' (1986) formation of rules for the classification of indirect threats, Al-Shorafat (1988) argues that a logical flaw exists in applying a formula designed for requests to threats as they are two different speech acts with fundamentally different functions. Further analysis of indirect threats in relation to Gingiss' (1986) criteria is provided by Yamanaka (1995), who argues that aspects such as the reference to the time of an action (point 'b' in Gingiss' (1986) classification) alone would rarely constitute a threat. Yamanaka (1995: 52) states that any criteria for defining indirect threats should be grounded in a set of criteria for defining direct threats, and proposes the following:

> *If A makes an assertion to B (not necessarily explicitly or in a declarative sentence) about.*
>
> **a.** *A's ability to carry out an action X*
> **b.** *A's intention to carry out an action X*
> **c.** *the consequences of performing an action X or of a previously performed similar action Y*
> **d.** *the occurrence of an action X in the near future*
> **e.** *A's suspending of an action X in return for the satisfaction of A's demands of B and all other preconditions for a threat are in effect, then A is heard as making a valid threat.* (Yamanaka, 1995: 52)

While this definition improves on Gingiss' (1986) criteria on account of a greater level of comprehensibility and a defined link to direct threats, it is difficult to envisage how it could be demonstrated that the conditions were upheld by a threatener unless they were stated explicitly. One way to therefore approach indirect threat analysis is to examine what an indirect threat, or a threat of any kind, does to a hearer rather than solely focussing on the speaker.

If it is accepted that threats are uttered to bring about a negative effect in a hearer, it can be argued that an indirect threat can only be a threat if it causes a negative psychological effect in either the recipient or in another hearer. Placing greater emphasis on bringing about a desired, unfavourable effect in a hearer also allows for contextual factors and so-called 'empty threats' to be factored into an analytical framework for threats. One such example discussed by Watt et al. (2016) is of a speaker stating '*I'm going to kill you*' to a friend who they have just beaten in a game of Scrabble. Here, the words form a direct threat, but it is unlikely that the utterance would bring about an unfavourable negative effect in the listener owing to the context in which it was made. A threat is therefore uttered but it is empty because it does not bring about an unfavourable effect in the hearer. More broadly, empty threats could be 'empty' due to several factors, including the surrounding context, or because it is clear to the addressee that the speaker is not capable of carrying out the threatened action.

Both Storey (1995) and Gales (2010) advocate for an approach which states that threats are bound by a relationship of shared understanding between speaker and hearer. Storey (1995: 75) argues that threats, by definition, are a two-way process and must be either accepted or acknowledged by a hearer to carry meaning. Gales (2010) also accepts this definition, arguing that 'threats are socially constructed acts of power between two parties – the threatener and the threatened' (Gales, 2010: 2). Milburn and Watman (1981: 7) also advocate a model for threats which places the listener in a key position, arguing that listeners modify the meaning of a given threat depending on both situational and individual factors, and therefore play an important role in both the meaning and interpretation of a threat. This proposition is further supported by Watt, Kelly and Llamas (2013: 100), who argue that for an indirect threat to achieve its desired effect, there must be shared understanding between speaker and hearer of both the content and context. This links to Storey's (1995) assertion that shared understanding between speaker and hearer is crucial for the successful communication of a threat, and further validates the idea that producing a desired, usually unfavourable, effect in the hearer is a key criterion in threat communication.

One distinction that can be proposed to better define the role of the speaker and the hearer in verbal threats is the difference between *making* a threat and *communicating* a threat. The emphasis is placed on not only making a threat, but communicating the intention behind an utterance to a hearer or target. Fraser (1998: 163) argues that aspects like ambiguity, a threat not being heard by the recipient or the recipient not understanding the words used within a threat can all serve as example of a threat being made, but not communicated. I would advocate for the expansion of this concept to include the acceptance or acknowledgement of the unfavourable effect of a threat on the recipient, as this would better define the importance of the listener's role within the interaction. In other words, the *making* of a threat only requires conditions on the part of the speaker, and relates solely to their intentions. However, for a threat to be *communicated*, the intended psychological effect on the recipient must be accepted or acknowledged by either that recipient or the hearer of the threat.

Consider, for example, a situation in which the status of an indirect threat is disputed in court, such as the dispute over whether Don Tyner threatened Vernon Hyde with the utterance 'How's David? [Hyde's son]', outlined by Shuy (1993: 108). Acting for the prosecution, a Federal Bureau of Investigation (FBI) analyst in this case stated that he considered the utterance to be a 'serious and real threat' (Shuy 1993: 109). However, contrasting linguistic analysis provided by an expert witness acting for the defence stated that the structure of the interaction and aspects of the surrounding context meant that the utterance should have been interpreted in its literal sense. This dispute therefore centred around the shared understanding between speaker and hearer over the communication of a potential indirect threat.

We know that when an utterance is produced by a speaker, the intended meaning is not always necessarily shared between speaker and hearer. A speaker can produce an utterance which results in the hearer perceiving a contrasting meaning to that which was originally intended. The notions of making and communicating a threat, along with the roles of the speaker and hearer in threatening communications, can be examined through this lens. Figure 1 shows four contrasting scenarios regarding the intention and interpretation of a potentially threatening utterance, based on similar work and categories proposed by Shuy (1993).

The contrasting scenarios in Figure 1 illustrate the potential outcomes of a threatening utterance, depending upon how the meaning is interpreted by the speaker and the hearer. The notions of making and communicating a threat can also be considered under this framework. In Scenario A, both speaker and hearer share acceptance of the utterance as a threat. Given that the speaker intends the utterance to be a threat and the hearer interprets it as a threat, it can be said a threat has been both successfully made and communicated. In Scenario B, the speaker does not intend the utterance as a threat, so a threat has not been

| SCENARIO A | SCENARIO B | SCENARIO C | SCENARIO D |
|---|---|---|---|
| The speaker intends the utterance to be a threat and the hearer interprets it as a threat. | The speaker does not intend the utterance to be a threat and the hearer does not interpret it as a threat. | The speaker intends the utterance to be a threat, but the hearer does not interpret it as a threat. | The speaker does not intend the utterance to be a threat, but the hearer interprets it as a threat. |

**Figure 1** Possibilities regarding the intention and interpretation
of a potential threat.

made, and the hearer does not interpret it as a threat, therefore a threat has not been communicated. In both Scenario A and Scenario B, the making and communication of the threat are consistent with one another. However, it is possible for mismatches to occur, as shown in Scenario C and Scenario D. In Scenario C, while the speaker intends the utterance to be a threat, the hearer does not interpret it as a threat. Under this scenario, a threat has been made but not communicated as it is not accepted as a threat by the hearer. The reverse applies to Scenario D, where the speaker does not intend the utterance to be a threat, but the hearer interprets it as a threat. Under this condition, it can be argued that a threat has been communicated, but not made.

Re-examining the 'How's David' example discussed by Shuy (1993), I argue that the dispute over whether the utterance was a threat was a contrast in interpretations between Scenario A and Scenario D. In this case, the prosecution argued for Scenario A, under which the speaker meant the utterance as a threat, and the defence argued for Scenario D, under which the speaker did not make a threat even though the hearer interpreted the utterance as a threat. Moreover, commenting on this particular case, Fraser (1998: 169) states that the court heard '[H]ow's David' as a serious threat. This highlights that in criminal trials where threats are disputed, the role of the speaker and hearer is reduced, with the perception and judgements of court-room triers of fact playing a pivotal role in the decision-making process. In such cases, a third-party listener bringing new perspectives and differing knowledge of the world to both the speaker and the hearer assumes primary responsibility for assessing and evaluating the intention behind an alleged threatening utterance. This is not wholly distinct from the idea of the 'reason-able person' interpretation discussed earlier, with the exception that jury trials are comprised of multiple people with a directive to achieve either a unanimous or majority agreement. Furthermore, the use of juries to make decisions about threats in courtrooms does not necessarily centre on the idea of an abstracted reasonable person, but rather on a juror's own knowledge and perspectives as well as the evidence and context provided as part of a trial.

## 2.4 Linguistic Analysis of Threatening Language

As stated in the introduction, linguistic analysis of threatening language is not a new phenomenon, although it is fair to say that research in the area has expanded in recent years. Gales (2010) argues that a large proportion of work conducted examining threats has focused on behavioural characteristics of the threatener rather than their use of language, and that there is still a lack of understanding about 'how threateners successfully threaten' (Gales, 2010: 2). This could be considered somewhat surprising given the status and classification of verbal threats as potentially serious language crimes. Furthermore, Gales (2010: 27) highlights that the majority of threats analysed by law enforcement agencies and threat assessment professionals are anonymous, leaving language as the main form of evidence which is available for analysis.

Gales (2015: 171) argues that while there is no one-to-one mapping between linguistic markers and actions taken by threateners, linguistic analysis of features such as stance markers can contribute greater understanding of threats and help to substantiate victims' claims of feeling afraid. A body of work on the role of stance markers in written threats has been conducted by Gales (2010, 2011, 2012, 2015, 2016). Stance is defined as the 'personal feelings, attitudes, value judgements or assessments' that speakers express through their utterances (Biber et al., 1999: 966). An investigation of grammatical stance markers in the Communicated Threat Assessment Reference Corpus (CTARC) is presented by Gales (2010). Gales (2010) reports, among other features, that the presence of the non-contracted modal verb 'will' was identified by both threat assessment professionals and non-linguistic scholars as a marker of an increased level of commitment to the threatened action, whereas the use of possibility modals such as 'may' weakened commitment and the speaker's overall stance. Nini (2017) further argues that prediction models such as 'will' emphasise certainty on the part of the threatener, and Napier and Mardigian (2003: 18) identified 'will' as a linguistic feature in high-level threats. However, a quantitative examination of stance markers in realised vs non-realised threats in the CTARC corpus is presented by Gales (2016), and shows differences in frequencies of use between the two groups including, but not limited to, prediction modals such as 'will' and 'shall' occurring more frequently in non-realised threats than realised threats, and certainty adverbs occurring more frequently in realised threats than non-realised threats.

Another larger-scale research project examining linguistic features of threatening language is presented by Muschalik (2018). This research examined linguistic features in a corpus of threats which were documented in legal texts, the Corpus of Judicial Opinions (CoJO). Muschalik's (2018) analysis focused on a collection of features which had previously been associated with threatening language. These features were conditional language, the demonstration of intention to commit an unfavourable future action, violent verbs, the stating of an agent of the threatened action, who the recipient of the threat is, use of personal pronouns, use of profanities and the mention of a weapon. Muschalik (2018) found that conditionality was relatively infrequent within the CoJO, with speakers more frequently using language which specifically referred to a future action, alongside violent verbs. Particularly usefully, Muschalik (2018) proposes the idea of a scale of explicitness for the analysis of spoken threats and argues that most of the threats in the CoJO were either extremely explicit in terms of the language features analysed, or extremely vague, with comparatively fewer threats containing a mix of both explicit and vague language features. However, Muschalik (2018: 181) states that despite these tendencies in the COJO data, 'there is no one standard way of realising a threat'.

While Muschalik's (2018) work provides incredibly useful advancement of knowledge around threatening language, there are some acknowledged limitations. The CoJO data contained a mix of spoken and written threats, with the vast majority of the spoken threats documented as a 'retelling' from the judicial opinion as opposed to being documented directly from the original source. Gales (2021) also highlights that Muschalik's (2018) work does not compare any potential differences between the spoken and written threats in the CoJO. Gales (2021: 215) argues that 'the investigation of spoken versus written registers of threatening communications is still an area in need of further exploration'. Muschalik (2018) also acknowledges that her study does not address issues surrounding the perception of threats, although she identifies this as a valuable area where more research can be conducted.

Gales' (2016) work shows how perceptions of features of 'threatening language' can often be at odds with the realities of the way that threats are uttered. For example, in the CTARC, threateners who acted on their threats were often found to use mitigating language to either displace responsibility or allow for negotiation to take place (Gales, 2016: 19). However, in an earlier community of practice survey among threat assessment researchers and practitioners, Gales (2010) found that mitigating language was often identified as a property of non-realised threats. This further illustrates the gap that can exist between the actual meaning behind a threat and the way it is interpreted, even by professionals and other experts. It also reinforces the potential differences between production and perceptual aspects of threat utterances.

Gales (2016: 21) further states that linguistic research on threats is yet to critically address potential differences between spoken and written threats. This includes research on stance markers. Biber et al. (1999: 967) argue that in addition to grammatical and lexical markers, speakers can display what they term a 'linguistically covert stance' through aspects of voice such as pitch, loudness and utterance duration. However, as the expression of what Biber et al. (1999: 967) term a 'linguistically covert stance' is not marked by grammatical or lexical aspects of speech but prosodic or suprasegmental features, listeners must instead infer the attitudes being expressed by the speaker (Biber et al., 1999: 967). This again shifts the analytic emphasis from speakers' productions onto listeners' perceptions of speakers' language use.

While Gales (2010: 58) discusses the potential for the inference of prosodic cues in written threats through aspects such as capitalisation, use of bold text or the use of emojis in computer mediated communication, prosodic factors remain a primary property of spoken language as opposed to written communication. Al-Shorafat (1988) explicitly argues for the inclusion of prosodic factors into a working set of conditions for defining spoken threats, although offers no further analysis about how this should take place, or which prosodic variables should be incorporated.

The relationship between prosodic or suprasegmental aspects of speech and the inference of threat in spoken language is, therefore, currently an under-explored area. Biber et al. (1999) do not present a detailed analysis of this aspect of communication, other than to state examples where fictional writers use dialogue tags such as '"Do you?" Helen spoke angrily' (Biber et al., 1999: 967), where the attached feeling is placed alongside speech marks to denote an attitude which would not be automatically marked by the words alone. Biber et al. (1999: 968) further add that readers have 'no difficulty in imagining the tone of voice and body gestures that could accompany these attitudes', although offer no empirical analysis of the phonetic markers associated with any kind of tone of voice. This issue is addressed specifically by Watt, Kelly and Llamas (2013: 100), who state that a speaker's 'tone of voice' is the term used by the police, the courts and the general public to capture properties of the speech signal that listeners may use to infer threat. This term also appears in scholarly articles about threatening language. For example, Milburn and Watman (1981: 55) argue that 'if a threat is uttered in a warm and friendly tone of voice, what might otherwise have seemed hostile or fearsome may be perceived as being humorous and acceptable'. However, Watt, Kelly and Llamas (2013) highlight the minimal amount of empirical research that has been conducted on how specific phonetic variables may contribute to listener perceptions of this so-called 'threatening tone of voice'. Investigating this further, Watt, Kelly and Llamas (2013) found that listeners inferred greater levels of threat from productions of the indirect threat '*I know where you live*' when it had been designed by the speaker to sound threatening, compared with productions of the same sentence that had been designed by the speaker to convey no threat or intent-to-harm. Watt, Kelly and Llamas' (2013) study helps to illustrate that listeners can use multiple channels when inferring threat from spoken utterances. However, they acknowledge that their work does not begin to analyse how specific phonetic cues may cause listeners to infer greater or lesser levels of threat in a talker's utterance (Watt, Kelly and Llamas, 2013: 100).

In a follow-up experiment to Watt, Kelly and Llamas (2013), Kelly (2014) investigated the plausibility of finding common phonetic cues adopted by speakers when making verbal threats. This research found that, of the features and spoken threats investigated, there were no consistently significant phonetic differences between utterances designed to be interpreted neutrally and those designed as threats. Although changes were made by speakers when wishing to sound threatening, the manner of achieving such a 'threatening tone of voice' was not consistent across the sample of speakers. Kelly's (2014) findings suggest caution in assuming cross-speaker commonalities when considering the phonetic basis of a 'threatening tone of voice'. Considering the wide array of possible reasons why somebody might choose to make a verbal threat, Kelly's (2014) results are not surprising, and the conclusion calling for 'a less simplistic consideration of threatening language' (Kelly, 2014: 29) is a valuable assertion. Kelly's (2014) study also showed limited phonetic correlation between threat utterances and previously documented reports on phonetic cues to anger. However, results in Tompkinson (2016) showed strong correlations between perceptual listener ratings for how angry, aggressive and threatening speakers sounded when producing a range of simulated direct and indirect threat utterances. This highlights the lack of one-to-one correspondence between speakers' production and listeners' perceptions regarding phonetic aspects of spoken threats in a comparable way to the results presented by Gales (2010, 2016) when examining written threats.

Gales (2010) argues that assumed linguistic markers of threats, despite their potential inaccuracy, can become enregistered in the minds of listeners. This can lead to stereotypical assumptions being made about the nature of threatening language. These kinds of generalised stereotypes are not associated with one particular case, but rather embedded as an abstraction and then applied by listeners in new situations. Given the lack of direct correspondence between the linguistic patterns adopted by threateners and their subsequent actions (Gales, 2010: 262), relying on folk-linguistic assumptions of threateners' intent inferred by non-linguists through speakers' language is potentially dangerous. This is further commented on by Bojsen-Møller et al. (2020: 39), who summarise that ideologies about threatening language are not always consistent with research findings. Given this, the assumption that language users will simply 'know a threat when they hear one' (Gingiss, 1986: 153) should be seen as problematic for any purpose with legal implications or consequences.

It is clear however, that linguistic research into threats should avoid any temptation to move towards making assessments and judgements about a speaker's psychological state. I argue that this should be considered an issue in psychology and not something that should be commented on by linguists. Indeed, point 9 in the International Association for Forensic Phonetics and Acoustics' code of practice states that '[M]embers should not attempt to do psychological profiles or assessments of the sincerity of speakers.' This issue is discussed by Watt, Kelly and Llamas (2013: 103), who state that the role of their perceptual investigation into spoken threats was not to comment on speakers' sincerity or identify phonetic traits which may mark sincerity (see Kirchhübel, 2013), but rather to explore listeners' responses towards speech samples produced in both a 'threatening' and 'neutral' tone of voice. Of course, this approach relies on the speakers' abilities to produce utterances which convey such a difference. It also relies on the researchers trusting the simulation of intention behind the test utterances. However, the approach has the advantage of allowing researchers to explore human judgements about threatening language without performing psychological profiling of a 'typical threatener' from vocal cues. It also moves the question away from an attempt to identify whether it is possible to determine whether a threat is 'real' or not. As great as the desire to be able to use vocal cues to determine the true intention behind a threat may be, the context-driven nature of threats makes it impossible. It can almost be seen as a phonetic equivalent to 'fool's gold'. Worse still, the belief that this can be done (Bunn and Foxen, 2015) creates a potentially dangerous disconnect between linguists and non-linguists tasked with evaluating threats in real-world situations.

## 2.5 Towards a Threat Typology

Milburn and Watman (1981: 10) state that there are five important elements which all contribute to the system under which threats are communicated:

1. A medium of communication
2. A source
3. A target
4. An audience
5. A situational context

However, the complexity surrounding threats as a type of language crime means that further clarification of a threat typology is needed beyond the five points identified by Milburn and Watman (1981). Table 1 details five key criteria which I argue are essential for the communication of a verbal threat. These criteria are consistent with Storey (1995) and Gales (2010), who both argue that shared understanding between speakers and hearer is a requirement for the successful communication of any threat. The factors also aim to cover both linguistic and contextual issues which relate to verbal threats.

We can also consider how language use binds together the different factors listed in Table 1. For example, factor 2 relates to the role and position of the threatener within a given threat. The main linguistic feature encompassed within this is the use of either first person or third person pronouns by a threatener as the agent of the threatened action. The use of first-person pronouns would serve to position the threatener as the agent of a threat, whereas the use of third-person pronouns would position the threatener away from, or independent to, the threatened action. The use of first or third person pronouns could relate to either written or spoken threats, and also either direct, indirect or conditional threats. This is exemplified below, with (1a) and (1b) illustrating the difference in threatener position and pronominal usage in direct threats, (2a) and (2b) show the difference with indirect threats, and (3a) and (3b) exemplify the difference with conditional threats. In each set of hypothetical examples, (a) shows a threat where the threatener is the agent of the threatened action, whereas (b) shows a threat where the threatener is not the agent of the threatened action.

**(1a)** – *I'll break both of your legs for sleeping with my girlfriend.*

**(1b)** – *Your legs will be broken for sleeping with Gemma.*

**(2a)** – *I'm warning you about a bomb at York Station. It will go off this afternoon.*

**(2b)** – *There's a bomb at York Station. It will go off this afternoon.*

**(3a)** – *If you don't pay me the money I'm owed, I'll break both of your legs.*

**(3b)** – *If you don't pay £1000, both of your legs will be broken.*

Factors 4 and 5 in Table 1 relate to wider contextual factors which could also influence the interpretation of a potential threat. These contextual factors are distinct from the more linguistically orientated factors listed in factors 1, 2 and 3, but are nonetheless essential when considering how threats are made and communicated. Factor 4 details the different possible relationships between the threatener and the hearer. The first of these possible relationships is one where the threatener and the hearer both know each other. When threats are made and

**Table 1** Factors relevant to the communication of a spoken threat.

| Factor | Explanation |
| --- | --- |
| 1 – Directness and conditionality | This refers to whether the threat is either direct or indirect (see Gales, 2010), and whether there is a condition attached to the threat or not. |
| 2 – Role of the threatener | This factor considers the specific role of the threatener in relation to the threatened action. The threatener can either be the agent of the threatened action or deliver the threat on behalf of somebody else. There may also be no agent in the threat and no use of any pronouns to link the threatened action to a specific person or group. |
| 3 – Medium of communication | This primarily refers to whether a threat is spoken or written, and would also consider threats delivered in dual modality, such as a written threat which has been read aloud. |
| 4 – Relationship between speaker and hearer | This considers whether or not the speaker and hearer know each other. This can be a bidirectional relationship where the speaker and hearer both know each other or are strangers to each other. It can also be a one-dimensional relationship where one party is known by the other, but not vice versa. This aspect could also consider the nature and level of the personal relationship between threatener and recipient, such as the difference between two casual acquaintances or a married couple. |
| 5 – Surrounding contextual factors | There are a wide range of potential contextual factors which could influence threat communication, including:<br>– Links to wider background information, for example, known terrorist, environmental or political groups.<br>– The potential role of institutions such as hospitals, schools or emergency services.<br>– Reference to provable knowledge or truths.<br>– The speaker's knowledge and views.<br>– The hearer's knowledge and views.<br>It should be acknowledged that the different knowledge and views that each individual speaker and hearer has will likely affect the interpretation of a potentially threatening utterance. |

the speaker and hearer are familiar with one another, it is likely the case that the contextual information introduced as a product of the relationship between the speaker and hearer will play a greater role in the interpretation of a potentially threatening utterance. For example, if someone exclaims '*I'm going to punch your head in*' to their closest friend, the relationship between the speaker and the hearer could be sufficient to mitigate the threatening nature of the words used. However, if the same utterance was produced by a speaker to an unfamiliar hearer, the anonymous relationship between speaker and hearer would provide less contextual information to mitigate the interpretation of the utterance as a threat. Two further possibilities are detailed here with respect to the relationship between the speaker and hearer of a threat. The first is that the hearer knows the identity of the threatener but not vice versa, and the second is that the threatener knows the identity of the hearer but not vice versa. The latter would likely be the type of relationship seen in anonymous stalking cases involving threats, where a stalker threatens a victim who is familiar to them, but the identity of the stalker is not known to the victim.

Relating this to the idea of wider context, the relationship between speaker and hearer with respect to threats is further complicated when threats to institutions such as hospitals, schools or the emergency services are made. In these cases, it is likely that the speaker and hearer will be unfamiliar with one another. However, there is more contextual information introduced into the speaker-hearer relationship in cases involving threats to institutions because of the institution itself. For example, consider a series of bomb threats made to schools. If a speaker makes a targeted bomb threat to a school via telephone communication, it is unlikely, although not impossible, that the person who answers the telephone in the school reception will know the identity of the threatener. The fact that the threatener has targeted the school as an institution reduces the personal nature of the threat and therefore the interpretation is likely to be less affected by the direct relationship between speaker and hearer. In a situation such as this, the relationship between threatener and recipient is likely to be unequal, as the threatener would likely know the institution they were targeting, but the representative of that institution (the school receptionist) would probably not know the threatener.

These kinds of contextual factors are largely independent from the linguistic features of threatening utterances, but are, nonetheless, important to consider in any taxonomy for threats as a type of communicative language crime. Language use is bound and shaped by context, and therefore accounting for this in any typology of threatening communication is essential. A similar approach is adopted by Bojsen-Møller et al. (2020), who classify threats as part of a collection of 'illicit genres' which are designed to achieve negative societal goals. By viewing threats in this way, the authors bind together the linguistic realisations of threats with other contextual factors which can influence interpretations. Bojsen-Møller et al. (2020) specifically argue that given the vague or ambiguous linguistic construction of indirect threats, contextual information is required for an indirect threat to be interpreted as a threat.

## 2.6 Summary

There are several key points that this section has highlighted through a review of existing research on threatening language. Firstly, threats are a linguistically complex phenomenon which encompasses many different components. Secondly, listeners' perceptions of what constitutes a threatening utterance are as important as speaker-specific factors when determining the status of a threat. Thirdly, with regards to spoken threats, both *what* is said and the *way* in which it is said can contribute to the overall interpretation of a threat, but this requires further linguistic research. It also requires an acknowledgement that folk-linguistic and stereotypical assumptions about threats and threateners can problematically affect and skew listeners' perceptions. Fourthly, context is particularly important for the interpretation of indirect threats (Bojsen-Møller et al., 2020) and should be built into a typology for spoken threats. Finally, and perhaps most importantly, we cannot simply predict whether a threat is real or serious from current knowledge about linguistic and phonetic features of spoken threats alone, despite some non-linguistic assumptions that this can be done.

## 3 Analysing Threat Production: A Corpus Approach

### 3.1 Introduction

The aim of this section is to present an introductory linguistic analysis of a new corpus of spoken threats. Drawing on previous research, I will also compare linguistic similarities and differences between this new corpus and previous linguistic analysis of written threats, as well as illustrate areas of similarity and divergence between threats delivered through writing and speech. This is particularly important given the lack of a body of research which critically addresses the differences between threats delivered in the two modalities. There is also a lack of research on spoken threats which focuses on examining authentic threats as opposed to simulated or experimental data (the relative merits of both approaches will be discussed further in Section 4). Linked to this has been the lack of an accessible corpus of spoken threats which is comparable to those built for the analysis of written threats such as CTARC (Gales, 2010) and the Malicious Forensic Texts corpus (Nini, 2017).

## 3.2 The Corpus of Spoken Threats (CoST)

A recent innovation which has facilitated this research is the development of the Corpus of Spoken Threats (CoST) (Tompkinson, Gales and Watt, 2021). CoST was developed through a collaborative research project between researchers at Hofstra University and the University of York. Ethical clearance for the project was obtained from the Department of Language and Linguistic Science at the University of York. The corpus contains transcribed and logged examples of spoken threats from publicly available sources. The threats in the corpus were recorded, and therefore do not rely on listener's memory or a re-telling of the utterance in the same way that many of the spoken threats analysed by Muschalik (2018) did. These recorded sources included, but were not limited to, websites such as YouTube, newspaper stories and social media. The corpus contains 978 instances of spoken threats. The collection was undertaken by a team of researchers working across both Hofstra University and the University of York, and there was no prescriptive search strategy other than using both external and in-site suggested links and keyword searches. A range of information was logged for each threat entry, including a link to the original URL, a summary of the threat and the background or surrounding context, whether the media source was a video or audio recording, information about the speaker(s) such as gender and approximate age, a transcript of the specific threat utterance, whether the threat was direct or indirect, whether there was conditionality embedded into the threat, other metadata including the date on which the entry was logged, and a unique sample number for every entry. Some videos and audio files contained multiple threat examples, and each of these were logged separately within the corpus.

Before I move to present the analysis of the CoST collection, it should firstly be acknowledged that the corpus is inherently 'messy' in nature. The goal of the CoST project was not designed to be selective in terms of the threats that were included, instead focussing on collecting a larger number of threat examples from a wide range of publicly available sources. Such a project will always relinquish a certain amount of control over the specific data examples, but the project was deliberately designed to be broad in scope in order to capture a wide range and larger number of spoken threats. The corpus was also cross-referenced and checked internally within the research team to ensure agreement existed on the tagging of information and the categorisation of threats. I took final responsibility for the inclusion of the threats in the corpus for the purpose of this analysis. Based on existing knowledge, CoST is the first and only corpus of its kind developed to specifically facilitate linguistic research on spoken threats. Building on initial work presented in Tompkinson, Gales and Watt (2021), the remainder of this section presents an initial outline of the contents of CoST, followed by an analysis of specific linguistic features that have previously been examined by researchers working on written threats. The two key questions that the section addresses are:

1. What is the linguistic composition of CoST in relation to previously analysed features of threatening language?
2. Are these features similar or different to those which have been documented as occurring in written threats?

## 3.3 Analysis

The following sections present numerical analyses of different linguistic features which have been previously identified in studies of threatening language. The analysis was largely conducted manually, with some additional analysis produced using Sketch Engine corpus analysis software.

CoST contains 978 examples of authentic spoken threats totalling 11,105 words. The overwhelming majority of threats were originally spoken in English, with US English (540 threats) and UK English (250 threats) the most commonly logged varieties. The majority of threats in CoST ($n$ = 784) were delivered by male speakers. Of the 978 authentic threats in the corpus, 928 were statements and 50 were questions.

### 3.3.1 Types of Threat

As previously discussed in Section 2, research on threats (see, e.g., Gales and Hurt, 2023) have used directness (direct vs indirect) and conditionality (conditional vs unconditional) as a way to categorise different threats. Following this approach, I have broken up the data in CoST into four categories: *direct unconditional, direct conditional, indirect unconditional* and *indirect conditional*. The classification of a threat as either direct or indirect was made based on whether the threatened action was overtly stated in the words used or not, and the conditionality classification was determined based on whether the wording of the threat stated a condition that could be upheld by the recipient to mitigate the threatened action. As discussed in Section 2, the concepts of direct and indirect threats are both useful and limiting at the same time. They are used here as an initial way of classifying the corpus entries and to provide comparable findings to existing written threat corpora. Examples for each type of threat are provided in Table 2.

**Table 2** Distribution of threat types in CoST.

| Type of threat | # of threats | % of CoST |
| --- | --- | --- |
| Direct unconditional | 463 | 47 |
| Direct conditional | 229 | 24 |
| Indirect unconditional | 243 | 25 |
| Indirect conditional | 43 | 4 |

The data in Table 2 show that 71 per cent of all the authentic threat entries in CoST were direct threats, and that around two thirds of the direct threats were unconditional. In contrast, a much smaller proportion of the corpus comprised indirect threats, with the vast majority of these types of threats also being unconditional. In total, more than two-thirds of the threats within CoST did not contain a conditionality clause.

Another way to examine the types of threat within CoST is to focus on the type of action being threatened. Table 3 shows the composition of CoST by the types of threatened actions. Given the variable and wide-ranging nature of the kinds of things that speakers can threaten, these are grouped into five broad categories: threats to kill, threats to commit violent or physical action, threats of non-violent action, threats of law enforcement, and unclear threats. An utterance was labelled as a threat to kill if there was a specific reference to taking life, including threats of suicide. An utterance was labelled as a threat of violent or physical action if it contained any reference to the threatener or a third-party committing any violent or physical act towards either the hearer or another victim. This category included threats to commit serious harm including stabbing and shooting, threats made by police officers to release a dog towards a suspect, threats of physical violence towards people such as punching, fighting and kicking, and threats to commit damage to property or possessions. By contrast, threats of non-violent action included threats to take somebody's job or remove their employment, enact lawsuits and disclose personal information. Threats of law enforcement included any utterance where a threat concerning arrest, legal detention or passing infor-mation to a law enforcement agency was made. Finally, there was a group of threats in the corpus which could not be classified into any of these groups and where therefore labelled as 'unclear'.

Table 3 shows that over half of the threats in CoST were threats of violent or physical action. There was a similar number of threats to kill and unclear threats, and there was a comparatively smaller number of threats of law enforcement and threats of non-violent action.

**Table 3** Distribution of threatened actions in CoST.

| Threatened action | # of threats | % of CoST |
|---|---|---|
| Threat to kill | 175 | 18 |
| Threat of violent/physical action | 513 | 53 |
| Threat of non-violent action | 43 | 4 |
| Threat of law enforcement | 59 | 6 |
| Unclear | 188 | 19 |

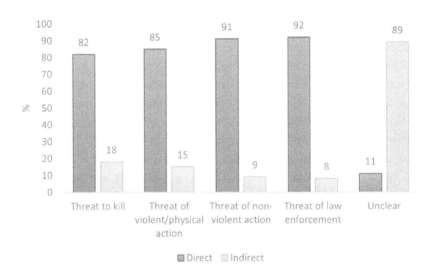

**Figure 2** Distribution of threatened actions and threat types in CoST.

One further pattern which can be explored within CoST is the relationship between threat type (as seen in Table 2) and threatened actions (as seen in Table 3). Figure 2 shows the number of threats within each 'threatened action' category broken down into the number of direct and indirect threats within each category. For the purpose of this analysis and for the sake of simplicity, conditionality was not considered separately. Direct conditional and direct unconditional threats were grouped into a single 'direct' category, and indirect conditional and indirect unconditional threats were grouped into a single 'indirect' category. The data in Figure 2 clearly show the nature of the difference between indirect and direct threats. The overwhelming majority of threats in the indirect category fell into the 'unclear' group, with the opposite pattern showing for the other 'threatened action' categories.

The data in Figure 2 illustrate that, unsurprisingly, there was a clear link between indirectness and an unclear threatened action within the corpus. In the majority of cases where a threatener threatened a specific action, whether that be violent or non-violent, they did so directly. Contrastingly, where a threat was indirect, the threatened action was overwhelmingly likely to be unclear.

### 3.3.2 Use of Profanities

Analysis of the data in CoST shows that 37 per cent of threats in the corpus contained at least one profanity. Table 4 shows the number of profanities contained in each threat within the corpus. Table 4 illustrates that the majority of threats which contained profanities contained either one or two instances of a swearword, with less than 3 per cent of entries containing three or more profanities.

Further to the above analysis, we can also consider which profanities were most used in the threats in CoST, and also examine the function of those profanities within the CoST entries. An analysis of the use of swearwords within the 2014 Spoken British National Corpus by Love (2021) found that 'fuck' was the most used profanity among English speakers, followed by 'shit' and 'bloody'. For this analysis, Love (2021) grouped different variations of each profanity within one overarching category. For example, *fuck, fucking, fucker and motherfucker* were all grouped under the category labelled 'Fuck'. Taking a comparable approach, analysis shows that 'fuck' was also the most common profanity in CoST (324 instances) by an overwhelming margin, followed by 'bitch' (42 instances), 'ass' (35 instances) and 'shit' (21 instances). It should be acknowledged here that the combined use of both British and American English within CoST would have likely affected the use of different profanities and makes the results not directly comparable with those produced by Love (2021).

**Table 4** Number of profanities in each CoST entry.

| Profanity usage within each threat | # of CoST entries | % of corpus |
|---|---|---|
| No profanities | 621 | 63 |
| One profanity | 244 | 25 |
| Two profanities | 87 | 9 |
| Three profanities | 18 | 2 |
| Four profanities | 6 | <1 |
| Five profanities | 1 | <1 |
| Six profanities | 1 | <1 |

**Table 5** Functions of profanities in CoST.

| Function of profanity | # of profanities |
|---|---|
| Noun | 182 |
| Modify noun | 149 |
| Modify verb | 101 |
| Verb | 55 |
| Other/Unclear | 5 |

The function of the profanity use within CoST is broken down in Table 5. The results of this analysis show that only 21 per cent of all profanities are used to either modify or intensify a verb (the threatened action). The majority of profanities in the corpus are either nouns or used to modify a noun. The 'noun' category also includes a number of threats where a profanity was used as a direct insult.

### 3.3.3 Agency and Use of Pronouns

Within CoST, 74 per cent of threats had the threatener as the agent of the threatened action, with 26 per cent of threats having either no specific agent or an unclear agent. One key linguistic feature relating to this is the use of personal pronouns. There are 2066 instances of personal pronouns in CoST. This means that personal pronouns comprise 18 per cent of all words in the corpus. Figure 3 shows the percentage distribution of first, second and third personal pronouns in the corpus. Singular and plural personal pronouns are collated in Figure 3, as are subject and object personal pronouns.

The data show a high use of first and second person pronouns in comparison to third person pronouns. This aligns with the notion that spoken threats primarily reflect the relationship between a threatener and a direct recipient as opposed to third parties and other agencies. Furthermore, examining first person pronouns specifically, there were over thirteen times as many instances of first-person singular pronouns ($n = 955$) than first person plural pronouns ($n = 73$) in the data. Coupled with the high number of threats which had the threatener as the agent of a specific threatened action, the data illustrates that most of these spoken threats have a singular agent of a specific threatened action.

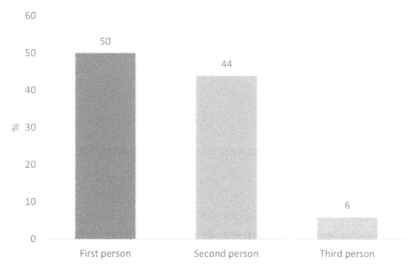

**Figure 3** Percentage distribution of personal pronouns in CoST.

### 3.3.4 Use of modal verbs

In Section 2, I outlined research which has highlighted that modal verbs are important in threatening communications as they convey the level of certainty towards the threatened action. Modal verbs such as 'will' have been identified as a marker of an increased level of perceived commitment and certainty to the threatened action, with those such as 'may' and 'might' weakening that perception of commitment (Gales, 2010; Nini, 2017). Following Biber et al. (1999), Gales (2010) outlines three categories of modal verbs in relation to written threats; possibility, prediction and necessity. Table 6 shows the numbers of modal verbs in the CoST data within each of these categories ($n$ = 822). Contracted forms of these modals are included alongside their full-form counterparts. For example, 'gonna' tokens are listed under 'going to', and 'I'll/he'll/she'll' tokens are listed under 'will'.

The data in Table 6 show that the majority of modal verbs in CoST are prediction modals, and these make up over 90 per cent of the modals used by speakers in the corpus. Based on previous assertions that predictions modals such as 'will' and 'going to' serve to increase perceived speaker commitment to a threatened action, it is perhaps unsurprising that this type of modal is the most common in CoST.

**Table 6** Distribution of modal verbs in CoST.

| Modal category | Modal | # of modals | % of modals |
|---|---|---|---|
| Prediction | Will | 457 | 56 |
| | Be going to | 274 | 34 |
| | Would | 25 | 3 |
| Possibility | Can | 32 | 4 |
| | Could | 5 | <1 |
| | Might | 5 | <1 |
| | May | 3 | <1 |
| Necessity | Have to | 13 | 2 |
| | Should | 4 | <1 |
| | Need to | 3 | <1 |
| | Must | 1 | <1 |

### 3.3.5 Comparing across Maximally Different Threat Types

In Section 2, I set out a framework for the analysis of threats containing five separate factors which should be considered. These were 1) the medium of communication, 2) directness and conditionality of the utterance, 3) the role of the threatener, 4) the relationship between speaker and hearer and 5) surrounding contextual factors. The data analysis in this section has examined the proportion of direct, indirect, conditional and unconditional threats within the corpus; looked at how many threats have the speaker as the agents of the threatened action; and examined profanity, pronoun and modal usage. However, the above analysis has not directly considered the role of context in CoST entries. One of the challenges with doing this is that, as previously explained, CoST is an inherently 'messy' dataset which contains a wide range of spoken threat examples from a wide range of different situations. It is therefore difficult to embed context into a broad analysis of the entire dataset. The exact situational context was not always fully available for each CoST entry and therefore context could not be systematically and sufficiently coded for within this analysis.

Despite being unable to undertake a systematic analysis of the influence of contextual factors on the language of the threats in CoST, further comparison between maximally different threat types can illustrate how the language used in spoken threats can differ within the corpus. This is an important step in considering the nuances and variation within CoST. Table 3 shows that the threats in CoST could be broken down into five threat categories: threats to kill ($n = 175$), threats of violent or physical action ($n = 513$), threats of non-violent action ($n = 43$), threats of law enforcement ($n = 59$) and threats in which the threatened action was unclear ($n = 188$). For the purpose of this section, I will focus on a comparison of threats to kill against threats where the threatened action was unclear. The rationale for this is that the comparison is between one very specific and serious type of threat against threats which are comparatively vaguer and more unclear. Additionally, 82 per cent of threats to kill in CoST were direct threats, whereas 89 per cent of unclear threats were indirect threats. Finally, there were a similar number of threats to kill ($n = 175$) and unclear threats ($n = 188$) within CoST. These three factors make the two categories particularly suitable for comparison. The following analysis looks at two key linguistic features analysed above for the whole dataset (use of profanities and use of modal verbs) within these two subsets of the data.

Table 7 shows the breakdown of modals within the two threat categories. There were more modals used in the threats to kill ($n = 161$) compared with the unclear threats ($n = 84$). The ratio of number of modals to number of threats was 0.92 for the threats to kill, but 0.47 for the unclear threats. However, the data in Table 7 show that although modals were more frequently used in the threats to kill, prediction modals overwhelmingly remained the most common type of modal in both categories, with comparatively negligible use of the other types of modals.

Table 8 shows the distribution of profanity usage within the two threat categories. Unlike for modals, the frequency of profanity usage in both threat categories was very similar. The total number of profanities used in the threats to kill was 86 (profanity to threat ratio of 0.49), and the total number in the unclear threats was 78 (profanity to threat ratio of 0.46).

**Table 7** Distribution of modals in threats to kill and unclear threats.

| Modal category | Modal | Threats to kill' | | 'Unclear threats' | |
|---|---|---|---|---|---|
| | | # | % | # | % |
| Prediction | Will | 97 | 60 | 33 | 39 |
| | Be going to | 44 | 27 | 38 | 45 |
| | Would | 6 | 4 | 1 | 1 |
| Possibility | Can | 2 | 1 | 5 | 6 |
| | Could | 2 | 1 | 2 | 2 |
| | Might | 4 | 2 | 1 | 1 |
| | May | 2 | 1 | 0 | 0 |
| Necessity | Have to | 0 | 0 | 3 | 4 |
| | Should | 3 | 2 | 1 | 1 |
| | Need to | 1 | 1 | 1 | 1 |
| | Must | 0 | 0 | 0 | 0 |

**Table 8** Distribution of profanities in threats to kill and unclear threats.

| Profanity usage within each threat | 'Threats to kill' | | 'Unclear threats' | |
|---|---|---|---|---|
| | # | % | # | % |
| No profanities | 117 | 67 | 134 | 71 |
| One profanity | 38 | 22 | 37 | 20 |
| Two profanities | 15 | 9 | 10 | 5 |
| Three profanities | 2 | 1 | 7 | 4 |
| Four profanities | 2 | 1 | 0 | 0 |
| Five profanities | 0 | 0 | 0 | 0 |
| Six profanities | 1 | 1 | 0 | 0 |

**Table 9** Function of profanities in threats to kill and unclear threats.

| Function of profanity | 'Threats to kill' | | 'Unclear threats' | |
|---|---|---|---|---|
| | # | % | # | % |
| Noun | 25 | 29 | 36 | 46 |
| Modify noun | 25 | 29 | 12 | 15 |
| Modify verb | 35 | 41 | 15 | 19 |
| Verb | 0 | 0 | 10 | 13 |
| Other/Unclear | 0 | 0 | 5 | 6 |

However, although the frequency of profanity usage was similar in the two categories, there were differences in the function of those profanities, as seen in Table 9. The data in Table 9 illustrate that, as was the case for the entirety of CoST, the most common function of profanities within the 'unclear threats' category was a noun, whereas in the threats to kill category, the most common function of profanities was to modify the threatened action. Equally, given that threats to kill require a verb which specifically denotes the taking of life, there were no uses of profanities as verbs in this threat category.

## 3.4 Comparisons with Research on Written Threats

Having presented an analysis of key linguistic features of spoken threats in CoST, this section will now turn to a discussion of the differences between the data in CoST and previous studies of corpora of written threats. The two main sources for comparison are the Communicated Threat Assessment Reference Corpus (Gales, 2010) and the Malicious Forensic Text corpus (Nini, 2017).

Both of these corpora contain collections of written threats and have been analysed extensively in published literature, and I will be referring to this literature for the comparative analysis in this section.

One initial key difference between CoST and the data in CTARC and the MFT corpus is the total size in words relative to the number of entries in each corpus. As previously stated, CoST contains 978 entries totalling 11,105 words. The mean average number of words per threat entry was eleven, with the shortest entry containing two words and the longest entry containing ninety words. By means of comparison, CTARC (Gales, 2010) contains 470 threatening communications from 139 authors totalling 152,000 words, and the MFT corpus (Nini, 2017) contains 104 written threat examples totalling 39,188 words. However, rather than this difference being caused by the register of the threatening utterance (spoken vs written), it is instead due to the ways in which the corpora were collected. Both CTARC and MFT included the full texts, whereas the entries in CoST only included the specific threatening utterance. This therefore makes the entries in CTARC and MFT inherently longer than those in CoST.

With regards to threat types, Gales (2010) reports that 62 per cent of CTARC was made up of indirect threats, with 26 per cent of threats in the corpus labelled as being conditional, and 12 per cent of the corpus comprising direct threats. CoST contains a notably higher number of direct threats than CTARC, where the majority of threats were indirect. However, the proportion of conditional threats is similar in both CoST (28 per cent) and CTARC (26 per cent). Furthermore, in Nini's (2017) collection of malicious forensic texts, there were only 2 examples of direct threats representing 4 per cent of the corpus.

There are two potential reasons as to why this difference might exist. The first is that the difference in the proportion of direct and indirect threats in the corpora could be linked to key differences between spoken and written language use. Spoken threats are largely momentary and delivered in real time between a hearer and listener. The only exception to this would be threats which are pre-recorded or delivered in the form of a voicemail message. However, written threats are permanent, and, in most cases, there is a delay between the writing of a threat and the delivery of that threat. Again, there are certain exceptions to this general rule, such as instant messaging chats, but it is true for most cases of written threats, and particularly those in CTARC which were collected before the rise in the use of instant messaging tools on mobile devices which has taken place over recent years. It could therefore be that the momentary nature of spoken threats, and particularly those delivered in 'real-time' between a threatener and a recipient, favours the use of more direct language in order to reduce ambiguity within that moment. Equally, the momentary nature of speech generally could also reflect a higher degree of spontaneity and a lack of pre-planning compared to written threats, or a lesser degree of conscious plausible deniability on the part of the threatener. This could also serve as a prompt for more direct language in spoken threats compared to those delivered in written form, where writers can edit and consider the words and phrases used over time.

It should also be acknowledged, however, that this difference could have occurred, or at least have been amplified, due to the different approaches to collecting the corpora. As Gales (2010) outlines, the CTARC collection contains authentic threats that were reported for investigation to a 'private behavioural analysis' group (Gales, 2010: 76) who deal with threat assessment. Gales (personal communication, 2023) explains that this behavioural analysis group – the Academy Group – received threats which had been escalated by other groups or individuals, such as local police forces or supervisors in workplaces. On this basis, these threats required additional or nuanced assessment and would more likely be indirect as a result of this. By contrast, CoST was collected using publicly available material from online sources. It could therefore be that an open-source search for spoken threats was more likely to skew results towards direct threats as opposed to indirect threats, despite the fact that 29 per cent of threats in CoST were indirect. It cannot be known for certain which of these reasons accounted for the difference in the number of direct threats in CTARC and CoST, but perhaps a realistic expectation would be that both elements contributed to the difference between the two corpora.

Comparing differences across types of threatened actions between CTARC, MFT and CoST is somewhat more challenging, as the categorisation of threats in the written threat corpora are slightly different to the above classifications. The CTARC data is classified into the overarching categories of *defamation, harassment, stalking, violence* and *other* (Gales, 2010), while Nini's (2017) MFT corpus is split into *violent act, extortion, spread malicious information* and *ransom*. Nini (2017) reports that 78 per cent of the MFT corpus is comprised of threats of violent acts, making this the most common category within the corpus. This is similar to the composition of CoST. By contrast, Gales reports that threats of violence represent just 9 per cent of CTARC. There does not appear to be a direct pattern here regarding the difference between written and spoken threats, but rather a reflection and acknowledgement that corpora such as CTARC, MFT and CoST, which contain real threats from real-world events, will likely contain inherent differences which will affect the data contained within them.

Initial preliminary research on pronominal usage in CoST has shown that personal pronouns occurred at a significantly higher rate in CoST than in comparable corpora of written threats, which include CTARC and MFT (Tompkinson, Gales and Watt, 2021). This again could be linked to the difference in the momentary or instant nature of spoken threats, where there is a more immediate need to establish the relationship between speaker and hearer. Equally, the difference could also be more simply as a result of the average length of spoken threats being much shorter than the written threats in CTARC and MFT, and therefore placing the roles of speaker and hearer more centrally within the spoken threat data.

Modal verbs have been previously noted as a key feature of threatening language as they underpin a speaker's perceived commitment to a threatened action. Analysis of the comparison of modal verbs in spoken and written threats was presented by Tompkinson, Gales and Watt (2021). This analysis illustrated that modals were used significantly more frequently in CoST than in the comparison Threatening English Language (TEL) corpus (Gales, Nini and Symonds, 2022). Within CoST, the prediction modals *will* and *be going to* occurred most frequently in the data. The use of 'will' as a frequently occurring modal in threats was also found by Gales (2010) in CTARC. However, the overall frequency of *will* usage in CoST is much higher, used at a rate of 41 instances per 1000 words compared to a rate of 6 instances per 1000 words in CTARC. Gales (2010) also found that for CTARC, 'can' and 'would' were the next most frequently used modals, whereas in CoST, the 'be going to' construction was used far more frequently than both 'can' and 'would'. This emphasises a difference in the relative use of modals between the two corpora, where certainty modals ('will' and 'be going to') occurred proportionately higher in CoST than in CTARC.

In addition to an analysis of CTARC, Gales (2010) also conducted a survey which aimed to assess people's assumptions about threatening language. One of the biggest disparities between the analysis of the threats in CTARC and the results of the survey was in the use of profanities. Gales (2010) found that 24 per cent of threats in CTARC contained profanities, whereas 73 per cent of those surveyed for their views on threatening language named profanities as a feature of threatening language. Analysis of the data in CoST shows that 37 per cent of threats contained at least one profanity. This was higher than the 24 per cent found in CTARC, but well below the 73 per cent from Gales' (2010) survey of ideologies around threatening language. This suggests that the disconnect between people's assumptions about threatening language is still detached from the actual realisations of spoken threats as well as written threats.

## 3.5 Discussion

The goal of the research in this section has been to outline the composition of CoST in relation to linguistic features which have been previously identified as being relevant to threatening language, and then to compare those features with previous research on written threats (e.g., Gales, 2010; Nini, 2017). In summary, the key findings are as follows:

– Personal pronouns are used more frequently in CoST than in comparable corpora of written threats.
– The prediction modal *will* was the most commonly occurring modal verb in both CoST and CTARC, but CTARC contained a higher proportion of possibility modals (particularly *can* and *would*) than occurred in CoST.
– The use of profanities was higher in CoST than in CTARC, but much lower than in Gales' (2010) survey of ideologies around threatening language.

The key question, however, is what does this add to existing knowledge about threatening language? Perhaps the most obvious conclusion that should be drawn from the analysis presented in this section is that research on threatening language should not assume that spoken and written threats are automatically comparable to one another. While this sounds like a simple assertion, it provides an important response to Gales' (2021: 215) warning that 'the investigation of spoken versus written registers of threatening communications is still an area in need of further exploration'. The results also show that even without considering the additional factors that contribute to differences between spoken and written language, like prosodic or paralinguistic cues in speech, there are still some linguistic differences between corpora of written threats and the spoken threats in CoST.

However, while the analysis in this section has highlighted some differences between spoken and written threats, this does not necessarily mean that *all* written threats are automatically different from *all* spoken threats. As previously stated, given the wide range of contexts in which threats can occur, alongside the variation in the method of delivery of both spoken and written threats, I would hypothesise that more than just the modality is likely to be influential in any comparison of spoken and written threats. I would argue that this should be the focus of future research in this area. For example, it would be interesting to assess whether controlling for word length would affect the linguistic composition of threats in corpora like CoST, CTARC and MFT. Equally, comparing collections of written threats delivered via social media platforms like Twitter with existing written and spoken threat corpora would be interesting, in order to assess whether written threats which may be delivered more 'instantly' are linguistically more comparable to spoken threats than the kinds of written threats which appear in corpora such as CTARC.

In summary, the research in this section should be viewed as a warning against automatically treating written and spoken threats as being comparable to one another. The discussion should serve to promote a more nuanced linguistic treatment of different types of both spoken and written threats in both modalities.

## 4 Analysing Threat Perception: An Experimental Approach

### 4.1 Introduction

The focus of the previous section was to compare features previously identified in written threats and assess how they compare to those in CoST. However, this only addresses one aspect of spoken threats, as it distils them down to the same linguistic components that are present in written threats. This section discusses how an experimental research approach can complement research on authentic threats, particularly with reference to how people perceive threat and intent-to-harm in the voices of others.

The communication of meaning through speech is not only about *what* someone says, but *how* something is said. It has previously been argued that linguistic features can become enregistered in the minds of listeners as markers of threatening language (Gales, 2010, 2016), and that a speaker's 'tone of voice' can influence threat perception (Watt, Kelly and Llamas, 2013). It is therefore entirely plausible to suggest that certain aspects of speech, or the way a threat is delivered, could influence people's judgements of how threatening a speaker sounds. As Watt, Kelly and Llamas (2013) illustrate, the so-called tone of voice that accompanies a particular threat can be an important part of the communication of meaning, yet there are few studies which specifically address the kinds of phonetic features which can be used by speakers to communicate aspects such as threat and intent-to-harm, or how aspects of people's voices can be used by listeners to infer threat from speech.

Despite this lack of threat-focussed research, studies stretching back over many decades have illustrated that listeners willingly form impressions of unknown speakers based on their vocal characteristics. Indeed, Pear (1931) and Allport and Cantril (1934) were among the earliest researchers to illustrate this phenomenon, using radio broadcasts to obtain listener evaluations of presenters' voices. Tusing and Dillard (2000: 148) argue that given their primitive origins, vocal cues may even have a more important role in social perception than either linguistic content or other non-verbal cues including, for example, facial characteristics or expressions. It seems unlikely that Tusing and

Dillard's (2000) assertion that vocal cues can be more important than verbal cues would hold for all kinds of threatening utterances, but equally unlikely that these vocal cues would play no part in influencing the communication of threatening utterances in certain contexts.

But how exactly is a 'tone of voice' achieved? And what cues in someone's voice might someone pick up on in order to infer meaning beyond that which can be obtained from only the words that are spoken, particularly in the context of threats? Of the phonetic parameters that have been investigated by researchers in relation to perceptions of attributes such as threat, dominance and aggression, along with various emotional states, Fundamental Frequency (F0) is the most common (Bachorowski, 1999; Ohala, 1984). Building on work by Morton (1977), who argued that lowered pitch marks aggression and dominance across a variety of animal species, Ohala (1984) showed that when listeners heard low pass filtered human speech with spectral details removed, low-pitched recordings were rated as sounding more dominant than high-pitched recordings when all other aspects remained constant. Ohala (1984) further argues that the lowering of mean pitch to signal dominance is related to the idea that lower pitch signals a larger person; a phenomenon known as either the 'frequency code' or 'size code' hypothesis.

In addition to F0, Laver (1994: 197) identifies that different phonation qualities can create both phonological and paralinguistic meaning, depending on both the particular quality and the conventions of the language in which it is being used. Gobl and Ni Chasaide (2003: 192) further posit that alongside stronger emotions such as anger, joy and fear, phonation and voice qualities can also signal milder states, moods, attitudes and feelings. Other phonetic features which have been shown to influence the signalling of emotions and affective states include speaking tempo (French et al, 2006), emphasis (Gussenhoven, 2004: 69), intonation (Scherer, 2003), voice quality (Laver, 1994; Gobl and Ni Chasaide, 2003), and regional accent (Bestelmeyer, 2019; Coupland and Bishop, 2007; Giles, 1970; Labov, 1972, Preston, 2002).

However, while the link between phonetic variables and the perception of affect, emotion and personal characteristics has been well researched, potential problems exist with making automatic links between this research and threat perception. This is highlighted by Kelly (2014: 7), who argues that attributing threats to certain psychological and/or emotional states is highly problematic. Kelly (2014) states that the goal of future linguistic research in this field should be to lessen reliance on such links, and I would agree with this approach. Watt, Kelly and Llamas (2013: 100) also discuss this issue, and while acknowledging likely links between anger and threat, they also note that 'we must avoid conflating angry speech with threatening speech', as 'wishing to threaten someone does not presuppose that the threatener is angry with the recipient' (or vice versa) (Watt, Kelly and Llamas, 2013: 100). Yet while this is true, we also have to acknowledge that there is a likely perceptual similarity between emotional states such as anger, and threatening language use, particularly in certain contexts. So, while links such as these should never be automatically assumed, we can use the literature on emotional speech to develop and test hypotheses for studies of threat perception in voices.

Chuenwattanapranithi et al. (2009: 3) argue that attempts to relate multiple acoustic aspects of the speech signal to different emotions has, as of yet, failed to create appropriate models of emotional speech. However, this approach contradicts research findings that have shown that humans can accurately detect emotion from vocal cues (Chuenwattanapranithi et al., 2009: 3). It can be argued that this imbalance between production and perception is appropriate for research on threatening speech. While it is unrealistic to claim that there are direct, one-to-one links between acoustic properties of speech and the production of threats (see Kelly, 2014), there may be more widely held perceptual properties which relate specific acoustic cues to perceptions of threats, as suggested by Ohala (1984). This further opens the possibility for the exploration of misconceptions related to what a 'typical threatener' sounds like, especially given Gales' (2010) assertion that supposed features of 'threatening language' become enregistered in the minds of listeners. This could link to the Danish case previously outlined in Section 2, where a threatener felt he had been treated unfairly because he had a deep voice and was therefore, in his opinion, automatically perceived as sounding as though he was angry when he was not.

So how should linguists set about addressing some of these issues through research? At the heart of this problem is speech perception and gaining an understanding about the effects that the way in which a threat is uttered can influence listeners' perceptions of the threatener. One approach that can be taken to address this issue, mirroring previous research on voice and speech perception, is the creation of experiments which test listeners' responses to various voices and utterances. While the analysis and use of real-world data such as the threats documented in CoST has the advantage of being authentic, this kind of data offers researchers little control when looking to explore and test responses to specific aspects of speech. In Section 3, I referred to CoST as being a highly useful but 'messy' tool, and it is this messiness which limits its scope for use in perception research. In real-world examples of spoken threat recordings, it can be difficult to ascertain ground-truth knowledge of speakers' backgrounds and the full context in which the recordings were made.

It is, of course, true that the evaluative settings in which research experiments are conducted are different to the kinds of real-world settings where legally relevant voice perception tasks take place, such as in a courtroom or another relevant earwitness environment. This is important to consider when applying such research to any real-world or specific contexts. However, using an experimental approach mirrors the approach taken in a range of research work on the perception of indirect threats (Watt, Kelly and Llamas, 2013), emotional trait perception, social trait perception and evaluative accent perception. The use of experimental stimuli also facilitates full researcher control over the variables being investigated, allowing for specific manipulations to be made and tested where necessary, and researcher choice over the appropriateness of both speakers and individual stimuli. This section showcases some examples of experimental research studies which were designed to test and advance ideas around how listeners infer threat from speaker's voices. These studies were conducted as part of my PhD research at the University of York, and full written versions of all the following experiments can be found in Tompkinson (2018), including further details about statistical analysis and methodological approaches. Collectively, they begin to address the issue of considering the impact of *how* a threat is uttered on listeners' perceptions, rather than solely examining the impact of *what* is being said.

## 4.2 Experiment 1: Exploring the Issue

The first experiment discussed here was designed primarily as a concept exploration test for the notion of whether experimental work could successfully explore the issue of how listeners infer threat from aspects of voice. In Experiment 1, forty listeners were presented with a series of utterances containing two indirect threats – '*I know where you live*' and '*I wouldn't do that if I were you*'. These target utterances were produced by a single speaker using a matched guise design, which created two contrasting speaker accent groups, but with both guises produced by a single speaker. No specific instructions were provided to the speaker about whether they should attempt to sound threatening or not. A non-standard London Cockney guise was used alongside a standard Received Pronunciation (RP) accent guise. The target stimuli were also altered to create contrasting mean fundamental frequency (F0) levels. Stimuli were resynthesised to create three mean F0 levels – low (90 Hz), mid (115 Hz) and high (140 Hz) using a Praat pitch alteration script (Fecher, 2015). The low and high values are 25 Hz above and below an approximation of an average male mean F0 level, as reported by various analysts (Hudson et al., 2007; Künzel, 1989; Lindh, 2006).

Within the experiment, listeners were asked to state where they thought the speaker was from. This was done to check the validity of the matched guise experiment and ensure that the target guises accurately represented the accents that they were designed to portray. The results of this part of the study showed that listeners generally identified the accent guises to appropriate regions. For the London Cockney guise, 74 per cent of responses identified voice as belonging to a speaker from London or the surrounding area, with a further 12 per cent of responses providing other accurate but less locally defined responses, such as *South England* and *England*. As RP is not a geographical accent, accuracy rates were slightly more difficult to quantify for descriptions of this guise. That being said, listeners generally located the RP guise to suitable areas of Southern England by providing either general responses such as *South England*, *England, the Home Counties* or specific counties such as *Kent* and *Surrey*.

The goal of the experiment was to assess whether F0 and speaker accent would influence listeners' judgements of how *threatening, aggressive, menacing, angry, agitated, friendly* and *intelligent* the matched guise stimuli sounded. Ratings were made using a seven-point Likert-type scale (1 = 'Not at all ... X', 7 = 'Very ... X'). Results showed that both mean F0 and speaker accent significantly affected listeners' threat evaluations. These effects were in the expected direction, with the low F0 stimuli rated as sounding the most threatening and the high F0 stimuli rated as sounding the least threatening. Additionally, the non-standard London Cockney accent guise was rated as sounding more threatening than the standard RP guise. This was expected following the results of previous accent evaluation studies (see, e.g., Dixon, Mahoney and Cocks, 2002), which illustrate that regional accents are often perceived more negatively than standard accents. It was also noteworthy that the effects for mean F0 and speaker accent were stronger for the utterance category which was rated as sounding less threatening overall (*'I wouldn't do that if I were you'*), suggesting that the more 'threat ambiguity' present in the words used, the higher the scope for characteristics of voice to be used by listeners to infer information about how threatening the speaker sounds.

The link between F0, perceived body size and perceived threat was also examined in Experiment 1. In addition to providing ratings of how threatening the speaker in each recording sounded, listeners were asked to provide evaluations of speakers' body size, with particular reference to height and build. These evaluations were made from vocal information alone as participants were not provided with images of speakers or any other visual cues to speakers' body size. The aim of this analysis was to further explore the previously associated link between F0 and body size perception (see, e.g., Ohala, 1984), and assess whether it would be extended to threat perception.

Results of the evaluations of speaker body size showed a trend for the guises with lower F0 to be perceived as having a larger body size in terms of both height and build. Speakers who were evaluated as being physically larger were also perceived as sounding more threatening. Finally, the experiment also showed strong positive correlations between listeners' judgements of threat and aggression, threat and menace, and threat and anger, as well as a moderate negative correlation between threat and friendliness ratings.

The results support the idea that supra-segmental aspects of speech (in this case, pitch variation), can combine with segmental phonetic aspects of speech (in this case, speaker accent) to influence perceptions of how threatening a speaker sounds. The findings lend support to the view that factors associated with both social and acoustic phonetic variation in the vocal channel are worthy of further exploration in work examining how listeners perceive threat in speakers' voices.

## 4.3 Experiment 2: Controlling for Variation in the Verbal Channel

Another concept exploration experiment, the design of the study in Experiment 2 adopted the approach taken by Watt, Kelly and Llamas (2013) in order to control for the interpretation of the verbal channel through the use of unfamiliar foreign language stimuli. The work presented in Experiment 2 further builds on Experiment 1 by examining the relative effects of three phonetic variables – *mean F0*, *speech rate* and *F0 range* – on listener threat evaluations of multiple speakers talking in unfamiliar languages. The stimuli for this experiment were produced by both male and female speakers. German and Polish speakers were used in this experiment, with alterations performed on the stimuli to create the required phonetic variation.

A Praat script (Antoniou, 2010) was initially used to alter the mean intensity level of all recordings to 70 dB. The recordings were then duplicated and altered to create contrasts for both F0 and speech rate. A Praat pitch alteration script (Fecher, 2015) was used to create two contrasting F0 levels for this experiment. For male speakers, the mean F0 of each recording was altered to 90 Hz (low) and 140 Hz (high), using the same rationale as the alteration used in Experiment 1. For female speakers, the mean F0 of each recording was altered to 170 Hz (low) and 250 Hz (high). These values are 40 Hz above and below an approximation of an average female F0 level and reflect the low and high ends of the mean F0 range reported for female speakers (Künzel, 1989; Traunmüller and Erickson, 1995). Following F0 alteration, the tempo of each recording was normalised to an articulation rate of five syllables per second, and subsequently tempo-altered ±20 per cent using Audacity software to create slow (−20 per cent) and fast (+20 per cent) speech rate versions of each stimulus. Performing the speech rate alterations in this way allows for tempo to be altered independently of average F0. Once all alterations had been made, each recording was re-checked to ensure that the F0 and speech rate were at the desired levels. All recordings were checked to ensure that no digital artefacts had influenced the sound quality as a result of the editing process. In addition to average F0 and speech rate, F0 range was also considered as a potentially influencing variable and was taken to represent a measure of how monotonous speakers sounded.

For the perception experiment, forty-two British English listeners completed an online survey where they were asked to evaluate how threatening they thought the speaker sounded in each recording using a 7-point Likert-type scale (1 = 'Not at all threatening', 7 = 'Very threatening'). Ten foil recordings were included in the experiment, interspersed between the target stimuli. Information was also collected on whether listeners had any background with foreign languages. To ensure that the verbal channel remained uninterpretable to listeners, any listener who stated they had any prior experience of German or Polish was removed from the sample beforehand, even if this experience only included basic learning at school. This method provides one way of enhancing the relative prominence of the vocal channel in relation to the verbal channel.

Results showed that both mean F0 and speech rate had a significant effect on listeners' threat evaluations. There was a trend for the low mean F0 recordings to be evaluated as sounding more threatening than their high F0 counterparts, and a bigger difference in threat ratings for the slow and fast recordings between the high and low F0 categories. The experiment also showed a difference in ratings assigned to male and female speakers, with the male speakers perceived to sound more threatening, and a difference in ratings assigned to the different languages, with the Polish utterances judged as sounding more threatening than the German utterances.

Watt, Kelly and Llamas (2013: 114) found no observable difference between induced-threat and neutral utterances that were played to listeners in unfamiliar foreign languages. However, the results in Experiment 2 indicate that listeners did assign greater or lesser levels of threat when specific phonetic parameters were altered in the speech signal, even when the signal contained words in unfamiliar languages. This highlights the possibility that there are certain phonetic parameters that British English listeners interpret as influencing per-ceptions of how threatening a speaker sounds, even in the absence of an interpretable verbal channel.

## 4.4 Experiment 3: Including an Experimental Context

Experiments 1 and 2 were designed as initial explorations of the notion that different aspects of speakers' voices could cause listeners to infer different levels of threat in those speakers' voices. However, as initial experiments, there were some notable limitations. One such limitation was that listeners were given no sense of any context in which the judgements they provided in Experiments 1 and 2 should be made. The third experiment outlined here addressed this weakness by examining whether providing experimental participants with contextual information would influence their evaluations of how threatening speakers sounded. The effect of different phonation qualities on listeners' evaluative judgements of how threatening speakers sounded was also tested, alongside differences in vocal pitch and speaking tempo.

The experimental design followed that of Experiment 2 by using unfamiliar foreign language stimuli. The stimuli used for the experiment presented in this section consisted of adapted versions of demonstration recordings produced by Hartwig Eckert in a standard North German accent for a reference work on voice quality types (Eckert and Laver, 1994). These recordings were in no way linked to the production of threats or a threatening tone of voice. The experimental stimuli were comprised of the same utterance produced using five contrasting voice qualities – *creak, falsetto, harsh, modal* and *whispery*. These were chosen as they span the frequency range adopted by male speakers (Laver, 1980) and have labels which are arguably more intuitive to lay-listeners than the labels for qualities such as laryngealized or velarized (Watt and Burns, 2012). The utterance produced by the speaker was '*Beim Fußball können die Sportfreunde immer davon ausgehen, dass die schönsten Tore und die interessantesten Spielzüge abends um zehn Uhr dreißig in der Sportschau übertragen werden*', which translates as '*With football, sports fans can always count on the finest goals and most interesting play being covered in the sports show at ten-thirty in the evening*' (translation provided by Watt and Burns, 2012). Watt and Burns (2012) point out that not all the recordings provided by Eckert and Laver (1994) contain labels, making it difficult for subsequent researchers to identify and use the recordings appropriately. Watt and Burns (2012) used the Vocal Profile Analysis scheme (MacKenzie Beck, 2005) to label each of the voice qualities provided by Eckert and Laver (1994), and these were independently verified by an independent phonetician with a high level of expertise in voice quality analysis (Watt, personal communication, 2017). In order to maintain consistency with previous research, the descriptive labels used by Watt and Burns (2012) were adopted in this experiment.

The voice quality stimuli were altered to create additional contrasts for both pitch and speech rate. This procedure was conducted using Audacity software. The 'change pitch' function was used to alter the pitch of each sound file by ±10 per cent to create higher-pitched (+10 per cent) and lower-pitched (−10 per cent) pitched stimuli for each recording. Following pitch alteration, each recording was subsequently tempo-altered ±10 per cent using Audacity to create slower (−10 per cent) and faster (+10 per cent) speech rate versions of each stimulus. All recordings were also checked to ensure that no digital artefacts had influenced the sound quality as a result of the editing process. Each recording was band-pass filtered between 300 and 3400 Hz to provide an approximate replication of the telephone channel frequency band. This was done in order to more accurately replicate the context in which stimuli were played to participants in the experiment.

A total of eighty participants provided informed consent to take part in a listening task in which they were required to answer a series of questions about the auditory stimuli outlined above. As the vocal stimuli were in German, listeners were asked to state whether they spoke German or had any experience with the language. Only participants who stated that they did not speak German and had either limited or no prior exposure to the language were included in the final sample. No participants had received any advanced-level formal training in phonetics.

One advantage of using foreign language stimuli in this experiment was that it allowed for analysis of how contextual evidence influences listener evaluations independently of an interpretable verbal channel. Participants were pre-assigned to one of two context groups. Group 1 were given prior instructions that the recordings they would hear were bomb threats received by German emergency service operators. Group 2 were given no contextual information about the origin of the recordings, other than to be made aware that listeners can be asked to provide information about unknown speakers' voices in forensic contexts. This was done to ground both experiments in some degree of forensic realism, but with the intention of only having one group who would explicitly associate the recordings they heard with threats. Listeners in both groups were instructed that the stimuli they would hear would be in German at the beginning of the experiment. This was designed to remove the potential for listeners to believe that the samples were taken from a language other than German, or that they would be exposed to more than one language in the experiment. Given the phonetic similarity between the German '*Fußball*' and English '*football*', listeners in Group 1 were informed that the bomb threat utterance they heard stated that a bomb would go off at a local football stadium. All listeners were provided with full information about the true nature of the recordings following completion of the experiment.

The results of this experiment showed that listener threat attributions were highest (most threatening) for the *harsh* voice quality and lowest (least threatening) for the *falsetto* voice quality. *Modal* voiced stimuli (the speaker's 'regular' voice) were rated as sounding comparatively less threatening than the *creak*, *whisper* and *harsh* recordings, but more threatening than the *falsetto* recordings. For all voice qualities aside from the *harsh* recordings, in which high threat ratings were provided by listeners in both experimental context groups, instructing listeners that they were evaluating bomb threats influenced threat attributions. Context had the biggest effect for the *whispery* voice stimuli, followed by the *modal* and *creaky* stimuli, the *falsetto* stimuli and finally the *harsh* stimuli. The effect for context was smallest in stimuli at both the higher and lower ends of the rating scale, and comparatively larger when threat ratings were closer to the middle of the scale. This can be seen in Figure 4.

Speech rate did not have a significant effect on listener threat ratings, with stimuli in the *slower* category not rated significantly differently from stimuli in the *faster* category. As previously outlined, pitch alterations were made relative to the five voice qualities tested in this experiment. The effect for pitch on listener threat ratings was therefore tested in interaction with voice quality, and this was a significant interaction. This effect is shown in Figure 5. In each of the voice qualities which contained vocal fold vibration (*creak*, *falsetto*, *harsh*, *modal*), the lower-pitched stimuli were rated as sounding more threatening than the higher-pitched stimuli. The opposite pattern is seen in the *whispery* voiced stimuli, with the 'higher-pitched' stimuli rated as sounding more threatening than the 'lower-pitched' stimuli.

It is clear that these experiments are highly artificial and abstracted from the realities of threats delivered by criminals and dealt with by the police and security services. But the purpose of running them was not to predict perceptual

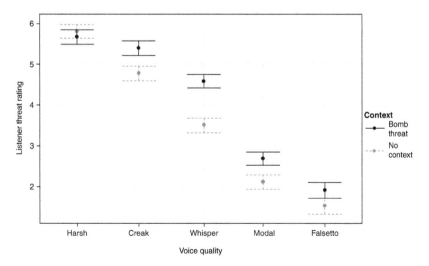

**Figure 4** Listener threat ratings for each voice quality in Experiment 3.

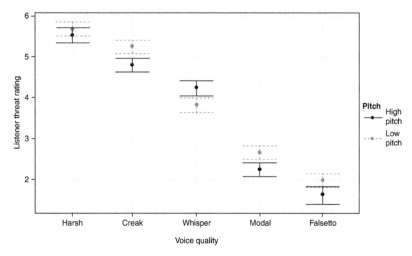

**Figure 5** Effect of pitch alterations on listener threat ratings for each voice quality.

responses in these kinds of contexts, but rather to establish whether there was a perceptual basis for these kinds of judgements around spoken threats. Without highly controlled experimental research, it is difficult to answer these kinds of questions. So, although this work is a large abstraction from reality, it was designed to underpin future research by testing base-level hypotheses about threat perception in a structured way.

## 4.5 Experiment 4: Linking Production and Perception

The experimental work discussed in the previous sections focussed entirely on perception. But of course, threats are bound by a link between production and perception, and this can also be explored and tested experimentally. The analysis presented in Experiment 4 focussed on speakers' own productions of what they considered to be a 'threatening tone of voice' (Watt, Kelly and Llamas, 2013). It also examined the effect of phonetic emphasis placed on realisations of the modal *will*, which have previously been linked to perceived markers of increased commitment on the part of threateners (Gales, 2010; Napier and Mardigian, 2003; Nini, 2017). Modals were also examined in some detail in Section 3 for the CoST data. The study firstly considered differences between speakers' productions of indirect threat utterances in what they considered to be a threatening tone of voice and a neutral tone of voice with respect to emphasis on the modal *will*. The extent to which this acted as a perceptual marker of threat for listeners was subsequently assessed. This extends the analysis in Section 3 by not just considering the presence or absence of the modal *will*, but also examining the phonetic delivery of that word in relation to the idea of a threatening tone of voice.

To create the stimuli for this study, twenty-seven speakers (nine male) were firstly instructed to read a neutral passage aloud, and then asked to familiarise themselves with a series of nine utterances. It should be acknowledged that there was a skew in this sample of speakers towards female speakers, which may not be representative of threats in real forensic contexts. However, it still allowed for interesting experimental findings to be produced. The neutral passage was a phonetically balanced text entitled 'Fern's Star Turn', with the set of utterances consisting of hypothetical, simulated threat utterances concerning a range of topics. These utterances are detailed in Table 10, in the order in which they were produced by the listeners.

The aim of requiring speakers to read a neutral passage in advance of producing the utterances in Table 10 was for them to become familiar with the recording procedure in advance of being asked to produce the threat stimuli. Once the speakers had familiarised themselves with the utterances in Table 10, they were asked to produce each utterance in what they considered to be a neutral tone of voice, and then again in what they considered to be a threatening tone of voice. This follows the experimental procedure used by Watt, Kelly and Llamas (2013) in their investigation of spoken threats. No guidance was provided by the researcher on which, if any, linguistic features should be altered by the speaker when they produced the two versions of each utterance, meaning that speakers were free to signal threat or neutrality in any way they felt was appropriate.

**Table 10** List of utterances recorded for the experiment.

| Number | Utterance |
| --- | --- |
| 1 | I know where you live |
| 2 | I wouldn't do that if I were you |
| 3 | Are you sure you want to do that? |
| 4 | When I get out of here, I'm going to do something about this |
| 5 | There's a bomb at York Station. It will go off this afternoon. |
| 6 | How's your mum at the moment? |
| 7 | Do you know there's a bomb at York Station set to go off this afternoon? |
| 8 | It gets really lonely around here at night |
| 9 | I'm warning you about a bomb at York Station which will go off this afternoon. |

As Table 10 shows, included within the nine utterances were the sentences, 'I'm warning you about a bomb at York Station, which will go off this afternoon' and 'There's a bomb at York Station which will go off this afternoon'. These utterances were used as target stimuli for the current investigation as the second clause in both utterances is a direct declarative which contains the modal verb *will*.

Measurements were made for mean F0, F0 range, speech rate and mean intensity in order to capture differences in pitch, tempo and loudness across each of the target utterances. In addition to this, measurements of mean F0, duration and mean intensity were also captured across each individual word within the utterances in order to assess the relevant phonetic cues to prominence. These measurements were taken based on previous assertions about F0, duration and intensity being key acoustic correlates of lexical prominence. These measurements were extracted using the ProsodyPro Praat script (Xu, 2013).

The results of this experiment showed two significant differences, in mean F0 and F0 range, between listeners' productions of utterances produced with a neutral tone of voice and utterances produced in a threatening tone of voice, with no significant effects for mean intensity or speech rate. There was a trend in the data for utterances produced in a threatening tone of voice to have a higher F0 range and higher mean F0 compared with those produced in a neutral tone of voice. This could be viewed as being at odds with perceptual results which showed that lowered F0 is associated with greater perceived threat. One reason for this finding could be that higher F0 and a greater F0 range can be seen as markers of increased vocal effort, which could have influenced productions of a threatening tone of voice. However, the disconnect between production and perception here is a relevant and interesting finding which is worthy of further exploration in future research.

The second part of the analysis in this experiment was designed to ascertain whether speakers would produce utterances in a threatening tone of voice with greater emphasis on the word *will*, given that previous research has linked the use of this token with increased levels of perceived threat (Gales, 2010; Napier and Mardigian, 2003; Nini, 2017). Results for this testing showed a significant difference in mean F0, mean intensity and duration of the *will* tokens between speakers' threatening and neutral productions of the two stimuli. The trend in the data was for a greater degree of phonetic emphasis to be placed on the word *will* in the threatening tone of voice productions with respect to the three measured variables, corresponding to higher intensity, higher F0 and a longer duration.

To further assess whether the previously described effects were confined to the word *will* or replicated for other words across the data, further testing was done to examine the differences in the phonetic prominence of other words between the threatening and neutral tone of voice productions of the two utterances used in the experiment. In this analysis, only the words that were present in both utterances were analysed, to ensure comparable testing with the *will* token. These words were *bomb, York, station, afternoon, this, go* and *off.* As was the case for *will,* mean F0 (Hz), mean intensity (dB) and duration (ms) measurements were compared for each word in each utterance. The results of this testing showed that there were no consistent patterns which would suggest that any other words in the two utterances tended to be realised by speakers with a greater degree of emphasis. There were isolated significant effects for the duration of the word *afternoon* and the intensity of the word *bomb*, but these were not consistent with significantly different realisations in F0 and intensity for *afternoon*, and F0 and intensity for *bomb*. This is unlike the results for the *will* tokens, which showed a significant difference between threatening and neutral tone of voice productions across the sample of speakers for all three of F0, intensity and duration.

Following the production analysis, a perceptual experiment was conducted to further investigate a potential perceptual association between phonetic emphasis on the modal verb *will* and listener inference of threat from speakers' voices. Utterances from six speakers were chosen from the larger data collection for use in the perceptual experiment. These six talkers were equally split in accordance with speaker sex (three male, three female). The utterance '*I'm warning you about a bomb at York Station, which will go off this afternoon*' was used. The six speakers were selected because they all placed greater emphasis on the *will* token in their threatening tone of voice production of the utterance compared with their neutral tone of voice production. Although *will* has been identified as a perceived marker of increased commitment to a threat (Gales, 2010; Nini, 2017), and the production analysis in this section showed significant phonetic differences between realisations of *will* in the threatening tone of voice and neutral tone of voice productions, no work has yet examined whether the degree to which *will* is emphasised in spoken threats causes listeners to infer greater threat to harm in speakers' voices. The choice of speakers for this experiment allowed for an assessment of whether the interaction between a previously identified lexical marker of increased threat and its phonetic realisation influenced listener attributions of how threatening speakers sounded.

A total of forty participants provided informed consent to take part in the perception experiment. They were instructed to listen to the auditory stimuli outlined above and then answer a series of questions about the utterances they had heard. All participants were recruited from the student population at the University of York and were either native British English speakers (33/40) or had native-like competency in English (7/40).

Participants were instructed that they would be exposed to a series of bomb threats that had been telephoned into emergency service operators. This context was designed to provide a more forensically realistic experimental context for participants. Participants were fully informed at the end of the experiment that the recordings were not real bomb threats. Listeners were asked to rate each voice for how intelligent, threatening and friendly they thought the speaker sounded using a seven-point Likert-type scale. Listeners were unfamiliar with the speakers they heard, had no prior formal phonetic training, and were not provided with such training in advance of the task.

As the recordings presented to listeners were taken from two contrasting 'tone of voice' groups, this analysis focussed on whether listeners would perceive differences between those utterances produced in a threatening tone of voice, compared to those which were produced in what the speaker considered to be a neutral tone of voice.

The analysis was conducted under the hypothesis that those utterances which had been produced in a threatening tone of voice by speakers would receive higher threat ratings from listeners than utterances produced in a neutral tone of voice. The results validated this hypothesis, showing a statistically significant difference between listener threat ratings for the threatening and neutral tone of voice utterances. The trend in the data was utterances spoken in a threatening tone of voice were rated as sounding more threatening by listeners. This effect is further illustrated in Figure 6, which plots listener threat ratings for the two 'tone of voice' groups. However,

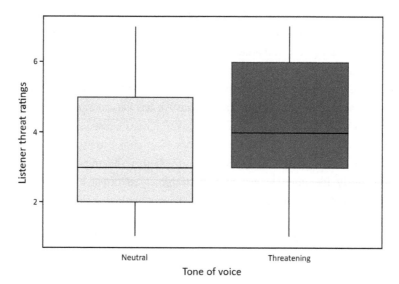

**Figure 6** Effect of 'tone of voice' on listener threat ratings. The plot displays the raw data distribution.

Figure 6 also shows that there is overlap between listener ratings in the two groups. This suggests that while the trend in the data showed that perceptions and productions were aligned, automaticity should not be assumed for every listener.

The analysis from this experiment contributes to the work of Napier and Mardigian (2003), Gales (2010) and Nini (2017), who all highlighted how the use of modal *will* can act as a perceived marker of increased threat within a potentially threatening utterance. The production analysis showed a trend for listeners to produce *will* tokens with greater phonetic emphasis in the threatening tone of voice utterances than the neutral tone of voice utterances with respect to the acoustic phonetic variables of F0, intensity and duration. The analysis showed significant differences between threatening and neutral tone of voice productions of the utterances '*There's a bomb at York Station. It will go off this afternoon*' and '*I'm warning you about a bomb at York Station which will go off this afternoon*' with respect to mean F0, duration and mean intensity across the will token. It can therefore be argued that when attempting to make their utterances sound more threatening, there was a significant trend in the data for speakers to place greater phonetic prominence on the word *will*. This trend was not replicated on other words which were shared between the two utterances used as experimental stimuli, which further highlights the relative uniqueness of the *will* tokens in these realisations.

However, this finding does not mean that courts should use the prominence of the word *will* to attempt to identify the level of threat in an utterance. There are several reasons for this. The first is that the utterances were produced in an artificial experimental context with the complete absence of any speaker intention to cause an unfavourable action. This is important because it differs from the context in which threats would be produced in real-world interactions. This does not mean that the findings of the experiment do not tell us something, but I would argue that it reveals more about threatening language ideology and stereotypes than it does about any potential real-world associations between linguistic markers and threatening language. With the absence of any real speaker intention, both speakers and listeners within the experiment were arguably reliant on their own ideologies and assumptions about what a threatening tone of voice would sound like, and this fed into both productions and perceptions. So, while it is true that had the speakers' 'tone of voice' not influenced listeners' judgements, then no difference in threat ratings would have been present between the two 'tone of voice' groups within the experiment, it is also true that the basis for this finding is more likely to have come from speakers and listeners drawing on their own assumptions or stereotypes about what a threatening tone of voice would sound like. Furthermore, Gales' (2010) findings which show that assumptions about threatening language can often be different from linguistic reality should underpin caution in using these experimental findings and directly applying them to real-world situations involving spoken threats.

## 4.6 Experiment 5: Expanding the Research Scope

The results discussed in this section are taken from a further threat perception experiment which is detailed in both Tompkinson et al. (2023) and Tompkinson and Watt (2018). To summarise, Experiment 5 followed the design of Experiment 4 and incorporated vocal stimuli from multiple speakers producing multiple indirect threat utterances. The same utterances used in Experiment 4 – 'There's a bomb at York Station which will go off this afternoon' and 'I'm warning you about a bomb at York Station which will go off this afternoon' – were re-recorded by different speakers for use in this experiment. Speakers were asked to produce each utterance twice, once where they emphasised the word 'will', and once where they emphasised the word 'this'. The experiment used speakers of three different varieties – Standard Southern British English, Northern Irish English, and foreign-accented English – to further test the findings from Experiment 1 that speaker accent can influence threat judgements. The effect of these variables, along with a range of other phonetic and linguistic variables on listeners' evaluations of both how threatening speakers sounded and how much intent-to-harm was conveyed through their speech was tested. These other variables included average F0, F0 range and the indirect threat utterance. The experiment also elicited perceptual judgements of pitch and speaking tempo from listeners. The effect of these measures on listeners' evaluative judgements of threat and intent-to-harm were also tested. The research also assessed the accuracy of listeners' judgements of pitch and speaker accent against measured acoustic correlates of pitch and ground truth knowledge of the speakers' accents respectively.

Analysis of the impact of the linguistic and phonetic variables on listeners' threat perceptions is discussed in Tompkinson et al. (2023). To summarise the findings, there was a significant effect for perceived pitch on listeners' evaluations of both threat and intent-to-harm, with a trend in the data for lower-pitched voices to be evaluated as sounding more threatening than higher-pitched voices. The results also showed that the effect was stronger for male speakers than for female speakers. With respect to the inference of threat and intent to harm, the other key finding from this study was the significant random effects of both speaker and listener, with the effect of listener being particularly strong. Through analysing 1000 random samples of 12 listeners, the number required to sit on a jury panel in the UK, a high level of individual variation was shown between the different listeners in the experiment. Average ranges sometimes spanned as much as

80 per cent of the scale available to listeners making judgements about speakers' voices. This result illustrated that listeners do not always agree about how threatening a given speaker sounds (Tompkinson et al., 2023). The results from the experiment also showed a strong correlation between listeners' judgements of how threatening speakers sounded and how much intent to harm was conveyed through their speech.

The second aspect of the study is presented in Tompkinson and Watt (2018), which focusses on the extent to which non-linguists can accurately assess linguistic features in voices. The analysis suggested that some listeners have the ability to assess vocal pitch in line with measured acoustic correlates, but others did not. A similar result was seen for the regional accent judgements, with those accents that were more geographically distant and/or unfamiliar being described less accurately. Furthermore, listeners assessments of speakers' body size were closely aligned to perceived pitch judgements in the expected direction, with lower pitched voices correlating with the perception of a larger speaker.

## 4.7 Discussion of Experimental Results

One of the most difficult balances to strike when evaluating the results of experimental research which could have forensic relevance is the balance between not understating the value of findings while also not implying that experimental results can be directly implemented in any real-world forensic scenario. I am not ashamed to say that this is an issue that I have found particularly difficult with regards to the results discussed both in this section and throughout the rest of this publication. On the one hand, the results presented in this section have shown that within the experiments conducted, different aspects of voices could influence listeners' judgements of how threatening speakers sounded. However, we should not overstate the value of some of these findings, particularly given the artificial experimental context with the absence of speaker intention to cause harm, alongside the finding discussed in Tompkinson et al. (2023) that there was a low level of agreement among listeners with regards to how threatening speakers sounded. Both of these outcomes should promote caution with the automatic application of these findings to specific scenarios or cases involving spoken threats.

So, what can we say about this research, and what issues should future work in this area address? Firstly, the experimental findings suggest that different aspects of voice at least have the potential to influence listeners' perceptions of how threatening a speaker sounds, and that these vocal parameters are among a series of factors, alongside the words spoken and the context, which can shape listeners' evaluations. However, the relative importance of these factors would likely differ on a case-by-case basis, should not be automatically assumed to hold for all listeners, and could be different according to the context in which a threat was both delivered and investigated. I would argue that if experimental research on threats were to be used in a specific case, the experiment should be specifically designed to reflect the specific circumstances of that case. As I outlined at the start of this Element, the research presented here is designed to be anticipatory rather than responsive (French and Watt, 2018). In other words, the experiments were not designed to provide findings which could be directly applied to specific cases, but instead to provide more general insights into issues around spoken threats. There could be situations where experimental research could specifically contribute to our understanding about particular issues in particular cases, but in order for findings to be directly applicable, the experiment should reflect the specific case circumstances as closely as possible. This would allow a transition from anticipatory research of the kind presented here, to responsive research which could be used in a specific legally relevant situation.

As discussed earlier, there is also a question about what information these perceptual experiments are tapping into when speakers are providing, and listeners are responding to, experimental threat stimuli. The connection between speakers' productions and listeners' perceptions of a threatening tone of voice was identified in Experiment 4, but I argue that this is far more closely linked to collective assumptions or stereotypes about language features as opposed to the actual reality of how speakers may or may not threaten. This argument is particularly applicable to experimental data given that there was no actual intention to commit harm on the part of speakers, only an attempt to make themselves sound more threatening. In other words, there is a key difference between the questions 'how do speakers attempt to simulate a threatening tone of voice?' and 'how do speakers produce threats?'. I would argue that both of these questions are interesting, but the first is much more applicable to the research presented in this section. From both a production and perception perspective, the results presented in this section are useful in exploring assumptions and stereotypes that speakers and listeners hold in relation to spoken threats, but given Gales' (2010) warning that these ideologies do not reflect reality for written threats, it would be unwise to conflate the two areas in relation to spoken threats.

While Al-Shorafat's (1988) assertion than prosodic factors should be included in the conditions for defining spoken threats is a worthwhile aim, it is also far from a simple task. I would argue that we are not yet in a position to explicitly include prosodic factors into any definitions of spoken threats, primarily owing to the small and restricted amount of research which has been conducted in this area to date. Future research on spoken threats should particularly focus on a mix of experimental, conceptual and realistic data to test and expand on some of the issues presented here.

Finally, I would argue that results of the kind discussed here should serve to promote caution over automatic associations and assumptions between threats and certain aspects of voice being used in investigations of spoken threat crimes. After all, factors such as the pitch of a speaker's voice or a speaker's accent do not objectively reflect a speaker's level of intent to cause harm, even if these features have the potential to influence listeners' evaluations. Furthermore, the wide variety of responses to the same voices by different listeners to voices in experimental contexts with either limited or no contextual information should also serve as a note of serious caution about real-world evaluations. If listeners do not agree in experimental evaluative settings, then it seems unrealistic to expect that they would do so in trial conditions. Based on the results of this work, it would be incorrect to assume that all listeners have the same evaluative biases of speakers' voices, and this is a potential danger if such biases are allowed to prevail over more objective evidence in cases involving spoken threats.

## 5 Concluding Thoughts

At the outset of this Element, I said I wanted to achieve three things. The first was to critically address the question of what threats are and how they work from a linguistic perspective. Secondly, I set out to address the similarities and differences between written and spoken threats using a corpus comparison approach. And finally, I wanted to explore the value of experimental research in this area, particularly in the field of perception of spoken threats. Each of these three aims has been addressed in a dedicated section of this Element.

To conclude, it goes without saying that threats are linguistically complex, multi-faceted and inherently linked to context. I argue that threats cannot simply be a product of the threatener, and instead require shared understanding of meaning between a listener and the threatener. This can be further complicated when the recipient of the threat is not the target, such as bomb threats delivered to emergency service call centres, or when members of juries are required to provide a third-party assessment of the meaning or intention behind a threat utterance. The analysis of the CoST data in Section 3 should provide a useful source of objectivity to guard against the assumptions that spoken and written threats are automatically equivalent to one another. And finally, the work in Section 4 showed both the strengths and limitations of using experimental research to investigate issues around how aspects of speech can influence the perception of threatening utterances.

This Element really does just provide a starting point for further research. Far from the previous sentence being something that I wrote in order to mitigate all the different types of research projects that could have been conducted in this area, I do genuinely see huge opportunities for further research. But it is my firm belief that in order to really understand how spoken threats work, researchers interested in linguistics, phonetics, text analysis, psychology, criminology, philosophy and law will be required to piece together their relevant expertise to solve problems and answer questions. This is particularly true for perceptual research, which is complex in nature and inherently holistic. My goals for this Element were to provide a foundation upon which more research can be conducted, and to perhaps also offer methodological frameworks which could be developed further through more research. I sincerely hope that the pages in this Element have achieved this aim.

## 5.1 Supplementary Materials

The CoST is available for research purposes upon request to the author. Please contact James Tompkinson at james.tompkinson@york.ac.uk.

# References

Allport, G. W. & Cantril, H. (1934). Judging personality from voice. *The Journal of Social Psychology*, *5*(1), 37–55.

Al-Shorafat, M. O. (1988). Indirect threats. *Word*, *39*(3), 225–7.

Antoniou, M. (2010). *Scale Intensity (Energy) with Output*. Northwestern University. Script for Praat.

Bachorowski, J. A. (1999). Vocal expression and perception of emotion. *Current Directions in Psychological Science*, *8*(2), 53–7.

BBC News. (2016). *EgyptAir Hijack: Man Surrenders at Larnaca Airport*. www .bbc.co.uk/news/world-middle-east-35915139. [Accessed 11 May 2023].

Bestelmeyer, P. E. G. (2019). Linguistic 'first impressions': Accents as a cue to person perception. In S. Früholz & P. Belin (Eds.), *The Oxford Handbook of Voice Perception*. Oxford University Press, pp. 667–82.

Biber, D., Johansson, S., Leech, G. et al. (1999). *Longman Grammar of Spoken and Written English* (Vol. 2). MIT Press.

Bojsen-Møller, M., Auken, S., Devitt, A. J., & Christensen, T. K. (2020). Illicit genres: The case of threatening communications. *Sakprosa*, *12*(1), 1–53.

Bunn & Foxen. (2015). *Forensic Language Analysis*. POSTnote Number 509. https://researchbriefings.parliament.uk/ResearchBriefing/Summary/POST-PN-0509 [Accessed 21 October 2022].

Chuenwattanapranithi, S., Xu, Y., Thipakorn, B., & Maneewongvatana, S. (2009). Encoding emotions in speech with the size code. *Phonetica*, *65*(4), 210–30.

Coulthard, M., Johnson, A., & Wright, D. (2017). *An Introduction to Forensic Linguistics: Language in Evidence*. Routledge.

Coupland, N. & Bishop, H. (2007). Ideologised values for British accents. *Journal of Sociolinguistics*, *11*(1), 74–93.

Danet, B., Hoffman, K. B., & Kermish, N. C. (1980). Threats to the life of the president: An analysis of linguistic issues. *Journal of Media Law and Practice*, *1*(2), 180–90.

Eckert, H. & Laver, J. (1994). *Menschen und ihre Stimmen: Aspekte der Vokalen Kommunikation*. Weinheim: Beltz Psychologie Verlags Union.

Fecher, N. (2015). *Praat Pitch Alteration Script*. Department of Language and Linguistics, University of York. Script for Praat.

Fraser, B. (1975). Warning and threatening. *Centrum*, *3*(2), 169–80.

Fraser, B. (1998). Threatening revisited. *International Journal of Speech, Language and the Law*, *5*(2), 159–73.

French, P. & Watt, D. (2018). Assessing research impact in forensic speech science casework. In D. McIntyre & H. Price (Eds.). *Applying Linguistics: Language and the Impact Agenda*. Oxford: Routledge.

French, P., Harrison, P., & Windsor Lewis, J. (2007). R v John Samuel humble: The Yorkshire ripper hoaxer trial. *International Journal of Speech Language and the Law*, *13*(2), 255–73.

Gales, T., Nini, A., & Symonds, E. (2022). *The Threatening English Language (TEL) Corpus (v1.0)* [Data set]. Zenodo. https://doi.org/10.5281/zenodo .6815671.

Gales, T. (2010). *Ideologies of Violence: A Corpus and Discourse Analytic Approach to Stance in Threatening Communications*. PhD Thesis. University Of California, Davis.

Gales, T. (2011). Identifying interpersonal stance in threatening discourse: An appraisal analysis. *Discourse Studies*, *13*(1), 27–46.

Gales, T. (2015). The stance of stalking: A corpus-based analysis of grammatical markers of stance in threatening communications. *Corpora*, 10(2), 171–200.

Gales, T. (2016). Threatening Stances: A corpus analysis of realized vs. non-realized threats. *Language and Law*, 2(2), 1–25.

Gales, T. (2021). Julia Muschalik, threatening in English: A mixed method approach (Pragmatics & Beyond 284). Amsterdam and Philadelphia: John Benjamins, 2018. Pp. xiv 246. ISBN 9789027256898. *English Language & Linguistics*, *25*(1), 211–17.

Gales, T. & Hurt, M. (2023). Linguistic analysis of disputed meanings: Threats. In C. Chapelle (Ed.). *The Encyclopedia of Applied Linguistics*. Wiley-Blackwell.

Giles, H. (1970). Evaluative reactions to accents. *Educational Review*, (22), 211–27.

Gingiss, P. (1986). Indirect threats. *Word*, *37*(3), 153–8.

Gobl, C. & Chasaide, A. N. (2003). The role of voice quality in communicating emotion, mood and attitude. *Speech communication*, *40*(1–2), 189–212.

Greenawalt, K. (1989). *Speech, Crime, and the Uses of Language*. Oxford: Oxford University Press.

Gussenhoven, C. (2004). *The Phonology of Tone and Intonation*. Cambridge: Cambridge University Press.

Hudson, T., De Jong, G., McDougall, K., Harrison, P., & Nolan, F. (2007). F0 statistics for 100 young male speakers of standard Southern British English. *Proceedings of the 16th International Congress of Phonetic Science*, Saarbrücken: Germany, pp. 1809–12.

Kaplan, J. P. (2016). Case report: Elonis v. United States. *International Journal of Speech, Language & the Law*, *23*(2), 275-92.

Kelly, S. (2014). *An Analysis of the Prosodic Properties of Neutrally-Worded Threat Productions*. MSc Dissertation, University of York.

Kelly, S. (2018). *Investigating the Phonetic and Linguistic Features Used by Speakers to Communicate an Intent to Harm*. PhD Dissertation. University of York.

Kirchhübel, C. (2013). *The Acoustic and Temporal Characteristics of Deceptive Speech*. PhD Thesis, University of York.

Künzel, H. J. (1989). How well does average fundamental frequency correlate with speaker height and weight? *Phonetica, 46*(1–3), 117–25.

Labov, W. (1972). *Sociolinguistic Patterns*. Philadelphia: University of Pennsylvania Press.

Labov, W. & Fanshel, D. (1977). *Therapeutic Discourse: Psychotherapy as Conversation*. Academic Press.

Larner, S. (2015). From intellectual challenges to established corpus techniques: Introduction to the special issue on forensic linguistics. *Corpora, 10*(2), 131–43.

Laver, J. (1980). *The Phonetic Description of Voice Quality*. Cambridge: Cambridge University Press.

Laver, J. (1994). *Principles of Phonetics*. New York: Cambridge University Press.

Law, J. & Martin, E. A. (2009). *Oxford Dictionary of Law* [7th ed.]. Oxford: Oxford University Press.

Lindh, J. (2006). Preliminary F0 statistics and forensic phonetics. *Proceedings of the 15th Annual International Association of Forensic Phonetics and Acoustics Conference*, Department of Linguistics, Göteborg University: Sweden.

Love, R. (2021). Swearing in informal spoken English: 1990s–2010s. *Text & Talk, 41*(5–6), 739–62.

Mackenzie Beck, J. (2007). *Vocal Profile Analysis Scheme: A User's Manual*. Edinburgh: Queen Margaret University College-QMUC, Speech Science Research Centre.

Milburn, T. W. & Watman, K. H. (1981). *On the Nature of Threat: A Social Psychological Analysis*. New York: Praeger.

Muschalik, J. (2018). *Threatening in English: A Mixed Method Approach*. Amsterdam: John Benjamins.

Nini, A. (2017). Register variation in malicious forensic texts. *International Journal of Speech, Language & the Law, 24*(1).

Nini, A. (2019). Corpus analysis in forensic linguistics. In Chapelle, C. A. (Ed.), *The Concise Encyclopedia of Applied Linguistics*. Hoboken: Wiley-Blackwell, pp. 313–20.

Ohala, J. J. (1984). An ethological perspective on common cross-language utilization of F0 of voice. *Phonetica, 41*(1), 1–16.

Pear, T. H. (1931). *Voice and Personality, as Applied to Radio Broadcasting.* Oxford: Wiley.

Preston, D. R. (2002). Language with an attitude. In J. K. Chambers, P. Trudgill, & N. Schilling-Estes (Eds). *The Handbook of Language Variation and Change.* Oxford: Blackwell, pp. 40–66.

Scherer, K. R. (2003). Vocal communication of emotion: A review of research paradigms. *Speech communication, 40*(1), 227–56.

Searle, J. R. (1979). *Expression and Meaning: Studies in the Theory of Speech Acts.* Cambridge: Cambridge University Press.

Shuy, R. W. (1993). *Language Crimes: The Use and Abuse of Language Evidence in the Courtroom.* Oxford: Blackwell.

Solan, L. M. & Tiersma, P. M. (2015). Threats. *Speaking of Language and Law: Conversations on the Work of Peter Tiersma,* 223–9.

Storey, K. (1995). The language of threats. *International Journal of Speech, Language and the Law. 2*(1), 74–80.

Tompkinson, J. (2016). *Accent Evaluation and the Perception of Spoken Threats.* MSc Dissertation. University of York.

Tompkinson, J. (2018). *Assessing the Influence of Phonetic Variation on the Perception of Spoken Threats.* PhD Thesis, University of York.

Tompkinson, J., Gales, T., & Watt, D. (2021). Investigating variation in threatening communication registers: A corpus analysis of written & spoken threats. *International Association of Forensic and Legal Linguistics conference,* Aston University.

Tompkinson, J., Mileva, M., Watt, D., & Burton, A. M. (2023). Perception of threat and intent to harm from vocal and facial cues. *Quarterly Journal of Experimental Psychology.* https://doi.org/10.1177/17470218231169952.

Traunmüller, H. & Eriksson, A. (1995). The frequency range of the voice fundamental in the speech of male and female adults. *Unpublished manuscript.* www2.ling.su.se/staff/hartmut/f0_m&f.pdf.

Tusing, K. J. & Dillard, J. P. (2000). The sounds of dominance. *Human Communication Research, 26,* 148–71.

Watt, D., & Burns, J. (2012). Verbal descriptions of voice quality differences among untrained listeners. *York Papers in Linguistics Series, 2,* 1–28.

Watt, D., Kelly, S., & Llamas, C. (2013). Inference of threat from neutrally-worded utterances in familiar and unfamiliar languages. *York Papers in Linguistics,* (13), 99–120.

Watt, D., Kelly, S., Tompkinson, J., & Weinberg, K. (2016) Anyone for menace? *Babel magazine, 14,* 18–23.

Xu, Y. (2013). ProsodyPro – A tool for large-scale systematic prosody analysis. *Proceedings of Tools and Resources for the Analysis of Speech Prosody (TRASP 2013)*, Aix-en-Provence, France. 7–10.

Yamanaka, N. (1995). On indirect threats. *International Journal for the Semiotics of Law, 8*(2), 37–52.

# Funding statement

The work presented in this Element was supported by funding from the Economic and Social Research Council [award no. 1500500], the Student Internship Bureau at the University of York, and Graduate Fellowship awards from Hofstra University. Research referred to in Section 4 was also supported by funding from the European Research Council under the European Union's Seventh Framework Programme.

# Acknowledgements

Although this Element has my name on the front cover, it would have never made it to print without the support of many talented colleagues. I particularly want to offer my sincere thanks and gratitude to the two anonymous reviewers who provided incredibly thoughtful and detailed feedback on this work. There is no debate that their contributions have improved this Element immeasurably. And of course, any mistakes which remain are my own.

The work I have discussed here was largely conducted during my time as a PhD student at the University of York. I remain eternally grateful to Professor Dominic Watt for first introducing me to the idea of conducting linguistic research on spoken threats, and for his continued guidance and support ever since. I also want to thank Professor Tammy Gales for her support during my research career. Echoes of Tammy's work are ever-present throughout this Element and her ideas have undoubtedly shaped and improved my thinking on this topic. Without Dom, Tammy, and our small army of student volunteers, the production of CoST would never have happened, and Section 3 of this Element would not exist. Working on that project during the COVID pandemic was a privilege, and it provided some much-needed academic escapism at a strange time.

I want to thank my current and former colleagues at the University of York, Aston Institute for Forensic Linguistics and J P French Associates for their support, ideas and friendship over the last decade or so. I consider myself extremely fortunate to have worked at all three of those institutions. I want to extend particular thanks to Peter French, Sarah Kelly, Jessica Wormald, Richard Rhodes, Katherine Earnshaw, Phil Harrison, Vince Hughes, Paul Foulkes, Tim Grant and Kate Haworth, who have all helped me become a better forensic linguist, speech analyst and researcher in the time we have worked together.

Finally, I dedicate this publication to my grandparents George and Diane. Although they might not always understand what my research is about, their love and support have helped me get to where I am now, and they mean more to me than they could ever possibly know.

Cambridge Elements ≡

# Forensic Linguistics

## Tim Grant

*Aston University*

Tim Grant is Professor of Forensic Linguistics, Director of the Aston Institute
for Forensic Linguistics, and past president of the International Association of Forensic
Linguists. His recent publications have focussed on online sexual abuse conversations
including Language and Online Identities: The Undercover Policing of Internet
Sexual Crime (with Nicci MacLeod, Cambridge, 2020).

Tim is one of the world's most experienced forensic linguistic practitioners and his
case work has involved the analysis of abusive and threatening communications
in many different contexts including investigations into sexual assault, stalking,
murder, and terrorism. He also makes regular media contributions including presenting
police appeals such as for the BBC Crimewatch programme.

## Tammy Gales

*Hofstra University*

Tammy Gales is an Associate Professor of Linguistics and the Director of Research
at the Institute for Forensic Linguistics, Threat Assessment, and Strategic Analysis at Hofstra
University, New York. She has served on the Executive Committee for the International
Association of Forensic Linguists (IAFL), is on the editorial board for the peer-reviewed
journals Applied Corpus Linguistics and Language and Law / Linguagem e Direito,
and is a member of the advisory board for the BYU Law and Corpus Linguistics group.
Her research interests cross the boundaries of forensic linguistics and language
and the law, with a primary focus on threatening communications. She has trained law
enforcement agents from agencies across Canada and the U.S. and has applied
her work to both criminal and civil cases.

## About the Series

*Elements in Forensic Linguistics* provides high-quality accessible writing, bringing
cutting-edge forensic linguistics to students and researchers as well as to practitioners in
law enforcement and law. Elements in the series range from descriptive linguistics
work, documenting a full range of legal and forensic texts and contexts; empirical
findings and methodological developments to enhance research, investigative advice,
and evidence for courts; and explorations into the theoretical and ethical
foundations of research and practice in forensic linguistics.

**Cambridge Elements** ☰

# Forensic Linguistics

## Elements in the Series